Excel

Basic Skills

English and Mathematics

Year 5
Ages 10–11

Get the Results You Want!

PASCAL PRESS

Contents

Introduction

The *Excel* **Basic Skills Workbook** series aims to build and reinforce basic skills in reading, comprehension and mathematics.

The series has eight English and Mathematics core books, one for each of the school years Kindergarten/Foundation to Year 7. These are supported by teaching books, which can be used if the student needs help in a particular area of study.

The structure of this book

This book has 30 carefully sequenced double-page units. Each unit has work on Number and Algebra, Measurement and Geometry, and Statistics and Probability in Maths, and Reading and Comprehension, Spelling and Vocabulary, and Grammar and Punctuation in English.

The student's competence in each of the 30 units can be recorded on the marking grid on pages 5 and 7. There are four end-of-term reviews. These are referred to as Tests 1 to 4. They assess the student's understanding of work covered during each term.

How to use this book

It is recommended that students complete each unit in the sequence provided because the knowledge and understanding developed in each unit is consolidated and practised in subsequent units. The workbook can be used to cover core classroom work. It can also be used to provide homework and consolidation activities.

All units are written so that particular questions deal with the same areas of learning in each unit. For example, question 1 is always on Number (addition) and question 11 is always on Measurement (time), and so on. Similarly in the English units question 1 is always on Reading and Comprehension, and question 14 is always on Punctuation. Question formatting is repeated throughout the workbook to support familiarity so that students can more readily deal with the Mathematics and English content.

The marking grids (see the examples on pages 4 and 6) are easy-to-use tools for recording students' progress. If you find that certain questions are repeatedly causing difficulties and errors, then there is a specific *Excel* **Basic/Advanced Skills Workbook** to help students fully revise that topic.

These are the teaching books of the series; they will take students through the topic step by step. The use of illustrations and diagrams, practice questions, and a straightforward and simple approach will make some of the most common problem areas of English and Mathematics easy to understand and master.

Sample Maths Marking Grid

If a student is consistently getting more than **one in five** questions wrong in any area, refer to the highlighted *Excel* **Basic/Advanced Skills** title. When marking answers on the grid, simply mark incorrect answers with 'X' in the appropriate box. This will result in a graphical representation of areas needing further work. An example has been done below for the first seven units. If a question has several parts, it should be counted as wrong if one or more mistakes are made.

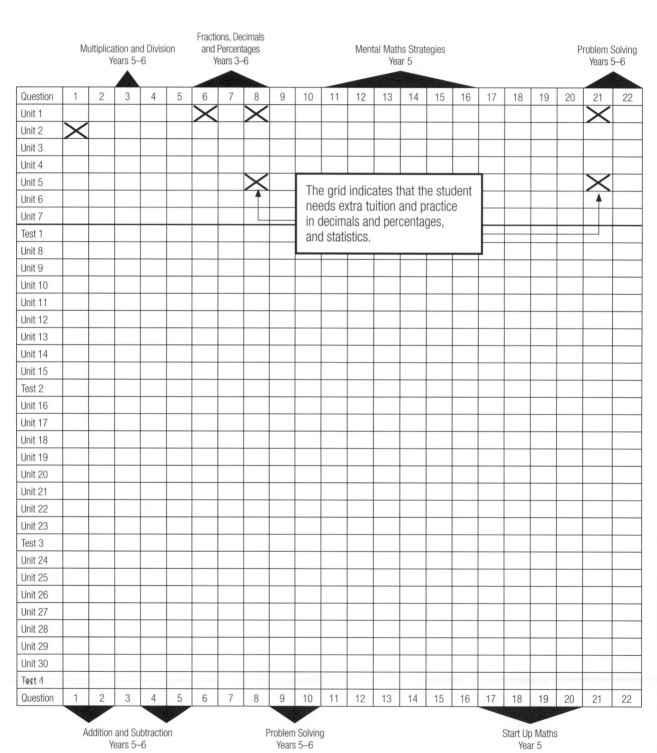

The grid indicates that the student needs extra tuition and practice in decimals and percentages, and statistics.

Maths Marking Grid

	Addition	Subtraction	Division/Multiplication	Place Value	Number Patterns	Fractions	Money	Decimals/Percentages	Estimating	Problem Solving	Time	Mass	Length/Perimeter	Area	Volume/Capacity	Temperature	2D and 3D Shapes	Angles	Symmetry/Transformation	Direction/Coordinates	Statistics	Probability
Question	1	2	3	4	5	6	7	8	9	10	11	12	13	14	15	16	17	18	19	20	21	22
Unit 1																						
Unit 2																						
Unit 3																						
Unit 4																						
Unit 5																						
Unit 6																						
Unit 7																						
Test 1																						
Unit 8																						
Unit 9																						
Unit 10																						
Unit 11																						
Unit 12																						
Unit 13																						
Unit 14																						
Unit 15																						
Test 2																						
Unit 16																						
Unit 17																						
Unit 18																						
Unit 19																						
Unit 20																						
Unit 21																						
Unit 22																						
Unit 23																						
Test 3																						
Unit 24																						
Unit 25																						
Unit 26																						
Unit 27																						
Unit 28																						
Unit 29																						
Unit 30																						
Test 4																						
Question	1	2	3	4	5	6	7	8	9	10	11	12	13	14	15	16	17	18	19	20	21	22

Sample English Marking Grid

If a student is consistently getting more than **one in five** questions wrong in any area, refer to the highlighted **Excel** Basic Skills title. When marking answers onto the grid, mark incorrect answers with 'X' in the appropriate box. This will result in a graphical representation of areas needing further work. An example has been done below for the first seven units.

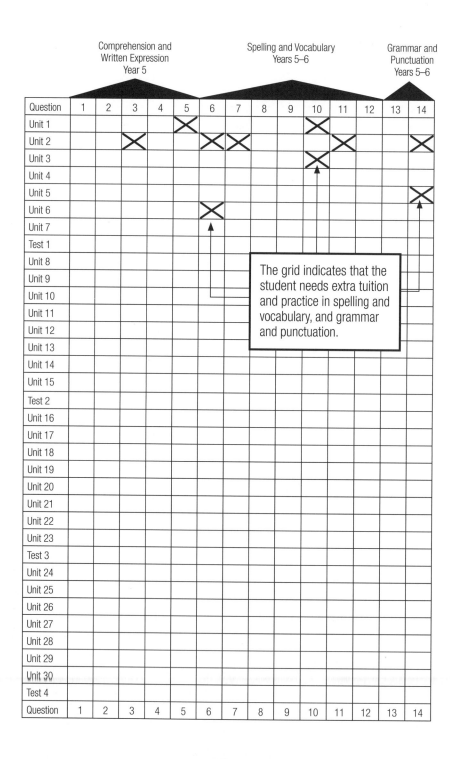

English Marking Grid

Question	Reading and Comprehension					Spelling and Vocabulary							Grammar and Punctuation	
	1	2	3	4	5	6	7	8	9	10	11	12	13	14
Unit 1														
Unit 2														
Unit 3														
Unit 4														
Unit 5														
Unit 6														
Unit 7														
Test 1														
Unit 8														
Unit 9														
Unit 10														
Unit 11														
Unit 12														
Unit 13														
Unit 14														
Unit 15														
Test 2														
Unit 16														
Unit 17														
Unit 18														
Unit 19														
Unit 20														
Unit 21														
Unit 22														
Unit 23														
Test 3														
Unit 24														
Unit 25														
Unit 26														
Unit 27														
Unit 28														
Unit 29														
Unit 30														
Test 4														
Question	1	2	3	4	5	6	7	8	9	10	11	12	13	14

Number and Algebra

1.

+	9	8	6	3	2	36
5						

2.

−	12	9	15	10	13	25
6						

3.

×	7	8	6	9	5	12
6						

4. How many thousands are there in 5864?

5. 568, 570, 572, ☐ , ☐

6. Write the fraction to show the shaded part.

7. 3×50 cent coins + 6×20 cent coins =

8. How many tenths in 0.56?

9. Round off 654 to the nearest hundred.

10. I have 47 sheep, 27 cows, 1 bull and 2 goats. How many animals have I?

Measurement and Geometry

11. What time (in analogue form) is shown on this clock?

12. The scale is balanced. What is the mass of the object?

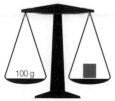

13. 2 m 69 cm = ☐ cm

14. How many square centimetres are in this shape?

   ☐ = 1 cm²

15. Write six hundred and fifty millilitres in short form.

16. Water freezes at 0 °C / 100 °C / 37 °C.

17. Name the shape that has 4 equal sides and 4 equal angles.

18. Which angle is a right angle?

19. How many axes of symmetry are there in a square?

20. **A   B   C   D   E   F   G**

A   Which letter is 2nd from the right?

B   Which letter is furthest left?

C   Name the middle letter.

Statistics and Probability

21.

How many trucks were sold?

22. Is it possible to throw a zero when you roll a die? Yes or no?

The hunt

During the Dreaming, a father and his two sons went kangaroo hunting. They came to a thickly wooded valley. Through it a river flowed, joining the sea. It was the cold, wet season. Suddenly it started hailing. Chunks of ice hurtled from the sky. The hunter and his sons ran for shelter to a cave. Seeing his children shivering and in distress, the hunter called on his ancestral spirit, Baiami.

The cave shook. Baiami appeared.

"Why am I called?" he thundered.

"My sons and I are freezing to death. Help us."

Baiami was the great ancestral spirit of the Cameraigal people. He had shaped the earth, and created the mountains, rivers and hills. He had made the animals and the human beings. Baiami took a hardened stick, sharpened one end and placed it into the knot of a rotted branch. Then rapidly twirling the stick between his hands, he made the softer wood smoulder. Glowing embers fell on the dried grass. He blew on them and the grass burst into flames. Baiami had created the first fire. The cave was filled with warmth and light. "Here is my gift to you," Baiami said. "Use it wisely."

Reading and Comprehension

1. How many were in the kangaroo hunt?

   _____

2. At which point in time does this story take place?

   _____

3. Baiami appeared because
   (a) the Cameraigal had called him.
   (b) they were freezing to death.
   (c) the boys' father called him.
   (d) the cave was where Baiami lived.

4. This story was used to explain
   (a) how humans learned to make fire.
   (b) what to do when it rains.
   (c) what gifts Baiami had to give.
   (d) the creation of the earth.

5. Number these sentences in order (1–4).
   (a) The grass burst into flames.
   (b) He took a hardened stick and some soft wood.
   (c) Glowing embers fell on the dried grass.
   (d) He rapidly twirled the hardened stick between his hands, making the soft wood smoulder.

Spelling and Vocabulary

Rewrite the misspelt words.

6. I saw it apear on the horizon. _____

7. Maria will never beleive this story. _____

Circle the word that has the nearest meaning to the underlined word.

8. Kim placed her name on the list.
   (a) saw   (b) put
   (c) said   (d) crossed

9. I nearly missed the bus.
   (a) always   (b) very
   (c) almost   (d) did

Circle the correct word in brackets.

10. Nothing could be (seen, scene) in the distance.

11. I can't afford to (lose, loose) my money.

12. She sat (sowing, sewing) near the window.

Grammar and Punctuation

13. Underline the **nouns** in this sentence.

    Apples, bananas, oranges and lemons were being loaded on trucks for the market.

14. Punctuate and capitalise this sentence.

    this is mr jp smith

    _____

Number and Algebra

1.

+	7	4	9	8	2	25
6						

2.

−	8	16	9	17	14	38
8						

3.

÷	6	4	2	10	8	16
1						

4. Write the number for five thousand and eighty-seven.

5. 1017, 1019, 1021, [ ] , [ ]

6. Colour $\frac{7}{10}$ of the shape.

7. What change do I get from $5 after spending $1.85?

8. Write in decimal form zero point two nine.

9. Is 4856 closer to 5000 or 4000?

10. Bill had $39. He spent $14.50. How much has he left?

Measurement and Geometry

11. Show five to two on this clock face.

12. The object I have has a mass of more than 100 g. Which scale gives a true picture?

A   B

C

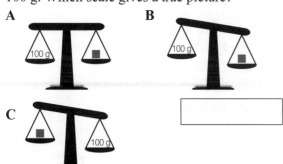

13. 428 cm = [ ] m [ ] cm

14. What is the area of this shape?

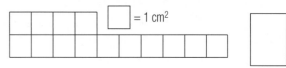

[ ] = 1 cm²

15.

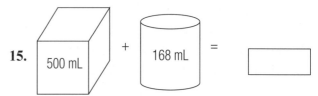

500 mL + 168 mL = [ ]

16. Name the instrument used to measure temperature.

17. Draw the shape I see if I look down upon the top of this shape.

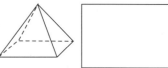

18. How many right angles are in this shape?

19. The diagonals of a rectangle are axes of symmetry. True or false?

20. If I am watching the sun rise, in what direction am I facing?

Statistics and Probability

21.

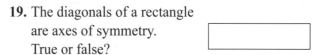

Which two have the same amount?

22. Which word best describes the chance of drawing a red marble from a bag of 20 red and 6 blue marbles? (impossible / unlikely / equal chance / very likely / certain)

Monday 10 April

Dear Diary,

I'm writing in the taxi on the way to the TV studio. It's 6:45 in the morning and it's just getting light. It was dark and cold when my alarm went off, and I wanted to stay in bed a little longer. Mum said, "No".

Mr Davis is driving me this morning. He doesn't talk much, which is good. I can write more. I can see the grass on the side of the road. It's still wet. It's supposed to be sunny later on. Let's hope so. I hate it when filming stops because of the rain.

My 'call' is for 7:30. Before we finish work every day we are all given a call sheet. It has all the information about what we'll be doing the next day, which scenes we'll be filming (or 'shooting' as they say), and what time everyone has to be at work. Under my name is 'Call time 7:30 am' and 'Scenes 4, 5 and 7'.

Hey, we're here already. I'll run out of the taxi as fast as I can and into the studio so I can stay warm.

Reading and Comprehension

1. What will halt filming?

   _____

2. The film being made will be shown on

   _____ .

3. What information is not on a call sheet?
   (a) which scenes are to be shot
   (b) the times people are required
   (c) people's names
   (d) the times they leave the studios

4. Mr Davis is
   (a) the author's name.
   (b) the author's father.
   (c) a friend of the author.
   (d) the taxi driver.

5. Number these sentences in order (1–4).
   (a) The sun is rising.
   (b) The alarm went off.
   (c) Mum made me get up.
   (d) The taxi arrived.

Spelling and Vocabulary

Rewrite the misspelt words.

6. I always have toast for brekfast. _____

7. It missed your head by a centimeter.

   _____

Circle the word that has the nearest meaning to the underlined word.

8. Mike ran <u>fast</u> towards the house.
   (a) quickly   (b) far
   (c) recklessly   (d) away

9. Dad <u>repaired</u> the can.
   (a) drove   (b) started
   (c) fixed   (d) examined

Circle the correct word in brackets.

10. I saw him (their, there).

11. We didn't see a (sole, soul).

12. He (wood, would) not do his work.

Grammar and Punctuation

13. Underline the **verbs** used in these sentences.

    Go away. Your dog jumps up. His muddy paws soil my clothes.

14. Punctuate and capitalise this sentence.

    the town of broken hill is in new south wales

    _____

    _____

Number and Algebra

1.
+	7	6	2	4	9	13
8						

2.
−	13	11	12	5	9	52
4						

3.
×	1	7	0	8	5	11
3						

4. Arrange these numbers from largest to smallest:
6911, 1691, 6191

5. 595, 596, 597, [   ] , [   ]

6. Write the fraction that means five out of 9 equal parts.

7. How many 5c coins equal $10?

8 Eight out of one hundred equal parts written as a decimal is:

9. 375 + 1588 is approximately equal to:

[   ] + [   ] = [   ]

10. There are 14 cartons in each box. If there are 9 boxes, how many cartons are there altogether?

Measurement and Geometry

11. What is the time 10 minutes after 5 to 11?

12. How many 200 g objects would have the same mass as 1 kilogram?

13. There are [   ] centimetres in 2 metres.

14. How many cm² are there in this shape?

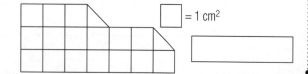

[   ] = 1 cm²

15. Which unit (mL or L) would you use to measure the volume of water in a sink?

16. Which of these thermometers shows the highest (hottest) temperature?

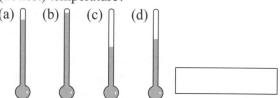

(a)   (b)   (c)   (d)

17. A square has [   ] sides, [   ] angles, [   ] diagonals, and [   ] axes of symmetry.

18. How many right angles are in this shape?

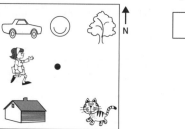

19. A regular pentagon has [   ] axes of symmetry.

20. What do I see in a north-westerly direction?

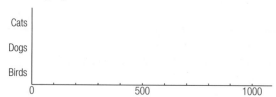

Statistics and Probability

21. On the Internet I found 836 references to cats, 977 to dogs and 238 to birds. Plot these numbers on the graph.

Cats

Dogs

Birds

0   500   1000

22. What are the chances of spinning a three using the spinning disc?

1 in 3,   1 in 2,   1 in 1
Circle your answer.

The curse of Tutankhamun

It was a hot November day, 1922 in the Valley of the Kings in Egypt. After years of searching, the archaeologist Howard Carter had finally found what he believed to be the resting place of the boy-king, Tutankhamun, who had been buried about the year 1000 BC—three thousand years ago.

In great excitement he sent a wire to his sponsor, Lord Carnarvon in England, so that he could be there when they opened the tomb.

Lord Carnarvon arrived soon after, and on 16 February 1923, they both broke through the door to find one of the most amazing archaeological discoveries of all time.

There were four rooms containing caskets, a gold throne inlaid with precious stones, gems, furniture, clothing and weapons. In the burial chamber itself, flanked by two black statues, were four gold shrines, one inside the other, and a nest of three coffins.

The inner one, of solid gold, held the mummified body of Tutankhamun, wrapped in a jewel-studded shroud. Over his face was a gold mask inlaid with precious stones.

Howard Carter and Lord Carnarvon were stunned by the splendour of their find, relics that are among the richest the world has ever seen.

They also found an inscription above the tomb, which they were able to translate. It read: *Death will come to those who disturb the sleep of the pharaohs.*

Reading and Comprehension

1. The tomb of Tutankhamun was found in
   (a) England.
   (b) the Valley of the Kings.
   (c) a pyramid.
   (d) Carnarvon.

2. Who was the discoverer of the tomb?
   (a) Tutankhamun   (b) Carnarvon
   (c) An Egyptian boy   (d) Howard Carter

3. Carter sent a *wire* to Lord Carnarvon. What must a *wire* be? _____

4. What metal was Tutankhamun's mask made of?

   _____

5. Number these events in order (1–4).
   (a) translating the inscription
   (b) finding the mummy
   (c) Lord Carnarvon joining Howard Carter
   (d) finding the many treasures

Spelling and Vocabulary

Rewrite the misspelt words.

6. I can't deside which one I like the best. _____

7. Put your coins away before you loose them. _____

Circle the word that has the nearest meaning to the underlined word.

8. Don't <u>lean</u> on the gate.
   (a) break   (b) push
   (c) rest   (d) climb

9. The bird flew <u>above</u> the roof.
   (a) around   (b) over
   (c) towards   (d) near

Circle the correct word in brackets.

10. (Tiers, Tears) came to his eyes.

11. I enjoyed listening to that (tale, tail).

12. Some people (horde, hoard) money.

Grammar and Punctuation

13. Put in the missing **pronouns**.

   "Oh no! _____ left _____ lunch at home," cried Lucia.

14. Punctuate and capitalise this sentence.

   tell fred i want to see him each friday in march

   _____

   _____

Mathematics

Number and Algebra

1.

+	1	5	3	7	9	74
7						

2.

−	8	3	10	5	9	70
1						

3.

÷	24	36	20	28	32	48
4						

4. Write the numeral shown on this abacus.

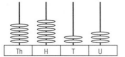

5. 3615, 3610, 3605, ____ , ____

6. What fraction is shaded?

7. $2 \times \$2 + 3 \times \$1 + 4 \times 50c$.
   Is this more/less than $10?

8. $\frac{7}{10}$ as a decimal is:

9. 99×8 is approximately equal to:

10. Share $3.65 equally between 5 children.

Measurement and Geometry

11. Show 6:27 on the clock face.

12. A jar of jelly beans has a mass of 1 kg. If the jar's mass is 250 g, what is the mass of the jelly beans?

13. What is the perimeter?

5 cm

3 cm

14. Calculate the shaded area.

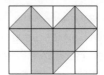 ☐ = 1 cm²

15.  This cylinder can hold 1 L.
    How much does it contain?

16. As the temperature goes up, the level of liquid in the tube will rise/fall?

17. A square-based pyramid has:
    ☐ rectangular faces, ☐ triangular faces, and ☐ square faces.

18. A regular pentagon has: ☐ equal sides and 5 ☐ angles.

19. Draw in the axes of symmetry in this triangle.

20. Put an X at (B, 3)
    Put a Y at (D, 1)

Statistics and Probability

21. Runs scored in a game:
    Mike |||| |||| ||||
    Jenny |||| |||| |||| |||| ||
    Juan |||| ||||

    How many more runs were scored by Jenny than by Juan?

22. What are the chances of this spinner landing on blue?

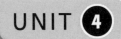

The history of false teeth

The earliest false teeth were probably used for decorative rather than practical reasons.

The ancient Egyptians believed that important people who died went on to an afterlife, so they would replace missing teeth in the mouths of dead kings to make them look nice in the next world. These teeth were lightly wired in place and could never have been used for chewing. Later, the Phoenicians (1000 BC–700 BC) made the first set of false teeth, held together with gold wire. The false teeth were carved from the teeth of oxen or other animals.

Throughout history people have tried to make false teeth that would work properly and look good. Dentists have always been quick to use the newest technology to improve their work. People who fixed teeth were not even called dentists in the olden days. Different people tried to do parts of the work that dentists do today. Priests, who believed that toothache was the work of evil spirits, prayed for the person to be freed from the curse of pain. Herbalists ground up strange mixtures to paint on teeth or feed to the sufferer. The local barber doubled as a dentist, and the local blacksmith, who was often very strong, used to pull out teeth.

Reading and Comprehension

1. Which group of people first experimented with false teeth? _____

2. Which metal was used centuries ago to hold false teeth in place? _____

3. The blacksmith at one time pulled people's teeth out because
   (a) he was strong.
   (b) he was the only one available to do it.
   (c) there were no dentists then.
   (d) he had the tools to do it.

4. People have tried to make false teeth so that
   (a) they worked well and looked good.
   (b) they were only decorative.
   (c) rich people could pay for them.
   (d) they would look good in the afterlife.

5. Match these professions with the work they did on teeth.
   (a) priests   (1) pulled out teeth
   (b) herbalists   (2) often worked as dentists as a second job
   (c) barbers   (3) made up mixtures to relieve pain
   (d) blacksmiths   (4) prayed to get rid of evil spirits

Spelling and Vocabulary

Rewrite the misspelt words.

6. Chocolate is my favorite flavour. _____

7. Mum's washing mashine is broken. _____

Circle the word that has the nearest meaning to the underlined word.

8. Will the <u>real</u> king come forward?
   (a) first   (b) young
   (c) rich   (d) true

9. Gina will <u>share</u> her lollies.
   (a) buy   (b) give away
   (c) bring   (d) divide

Circle the correct word in brackets.

10. The (dew, due) glistened on the grass.

11. (Where, Were) have you been?

12. It's over (there, their).

Grammar and Punctuation

13. Change these **nouns** to **pronouns**.
    Bill said that <u>Bill</u> had left <u>Bill's</u> pencil at home and could <u>the person saying this</u> lend <u>Bill</u> one.

14. Punctuate and capitalise this sentence.
    mum bought apples pears bananas and oranges from mr ling

    _____

    _____

Number and Algebra

1.

+	1	8	3	7	4	35
9						

2.

−	6	12	7	4	10	18
3						

3.

×	6	2	8	4	5	10
5						

4. What is the value of the 4 in 2487?

5. Count on in tens from 3578:

[ ] , [ ] , [ ]

6. Of 100 equal parts 63 are shaded. What fraction is unshaded?

7. What is the minimum number of coins for $2.65 change?

8. 66 hundredths as a decimal is:

9. Round off 2.48 to the nearest whole number.

10. I went shopping with a $50 note. I spent $18.50, then $3.20 and finally $12.25. How much have I left?

Measurement and Geometry

11. 20 past 7 in analogue form is the same as [ ] in digital form.

12. Write nine hundred and eighty-five grams as a numeral with a symbol.

13. Jack runs around the block twice. The block is 1 km long and 500 m wide. How far does he run?

14. What area of the rectangle is not shaded?

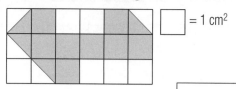

[ ] = 1 cm²

15. Bill bought a juice 'popper'. It held 250 mL / 250 L. Select the correct amount.

16. Water boils at 0 °C / 37 °C / 100 °C?

17. A regular octagon has [ ] diagonals and [ ] axes of symmetry.

18. Which angle is obtuse?

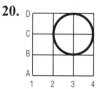

19. A regular polygon has six axes of symmetry. Name this shape.

20.

The coordinates of the centre of the circle are:

[,]

Statistics and Probability

21. This bar represents a total of $64.

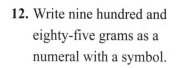

How much money has:

(a) Con? [ ] (b) Jenny? [ ]

(c) Lu? [ ]

22. I have a disc with six numbered sections. What are the chances of spinning a 4?

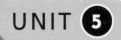

Rod Puppets

A rod puppet is an extension of the glove puppet. Its head and hands are fixed to the ends of sticks or rods, which the puppeteer uses to operate the figure from below. Rod puppets usually have no legs, but a cloth body that is either sewn or draped. The head and hands can be made from wood, cloth, papier-maché or plastic.

A disadvantage of the rod puppet is that its movements may be slow and limited, but it can be easily controlled. The best-known rod puppets are probably wayang golek puppets from Java in Indonesia, famous for their beauty.

Muppets are a combination of hand and rod puppets. The operator puts one hand in the puppet's head, to move the mouth. The other hand controls two rods that move the arms, either both at once or one at a time.

Reading and Comprehension

1. What is the disadvantage of rod puppets?

_____

2. What is the body of a rod puppet made of?

_____

3. Select the true statement.
   (a) Rod puppets are large hand puppets.
   (b) Rod puppets are made stiff with rods.
   (c) Rod puppets seldom have legs.
   (d) Rod puppets move quickly.

4. The rods of a rod puppet are fixed to
   (a) the head.
   (b) the body.
   (c) the legs.
   (d) the arms and head.

5. Number these facts about muppets in order (1–4).
   (a) The hand in the head controls the mouth.
   (b) One hand controls the head.
   (c) The rods control the hands of the muppet.
   (d) The other hand controls the rods.

Spelling and Vocabulary

Rewrite the misspelt words.

6. The ball went threw the pane of glass.

_____

7. Probabably you're right.

_____

Circle the word that has the nearest meaning to the underlined word.

8. After five minutes he had no <u>score</u> in the game.
   (a) result   (b) points
   (c) progress   (d) energy

9. The power lines began to <u>sway</u> in the breeze.
   (a) fall   (b) break
   (c) swing   (d) snap

Circle the correct word in brackets.

10. Have you (saw, seen) the camera?

11. He can (run, ran) like the wind.

12. The storm will (break, brake) soon.

Grammar and Punctuation

13. Rewrite this sentence using different **verbs**.

    Raynor <u>got</u> out of the bed, <u>got</u> dressed, <u>got</u> his lunch and <u>got</u> the bus to school.

    _____

    _____

14. Punctuate and capitalise this sentence.

    is your teacher mr ck perry

    _____

Number and Algebra

1.

+	8	6	5	9	3	89
1						

2.

−	11	6	4	8	7	22
2						

3.

÷	42	56	28	63	49	84
7						

4. Write 2864 in words.

5. Count backwards from 1836 in hundreds.

☐ , ☐ , ☐

6. Draw 10 equal parts. Shade $\frac{3}{10}$.

7. I had $20. I spent $9.45. How much have I now?

8. If 0.7 is shaded, what decimal fraction is unshaded?

9. Round off 5751 to the nearest thousand.

10. The bus leaves at 9:03 am. I get to the bus stop at 8:47 am. How long do I wait?

Measurement and Geometry

11. is the same as **10:47**

12. Write 728 kg in words.

13.  The perimeter of this triangle is:

8 m 8 m
8 m

14. What area is:
(a) shaded?

(b) unshaded?

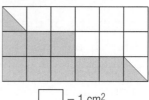

☐ = 1 cm²

15. I counted 2 × 2 L, 3 × 1 L and 2 × 600 mL cartons of milk. What is the total in millilitres?

16. The maximum temperature today was 28 °C and the minimum 16 °C. What was the difference?

17. In Greek *hept* means 7 and *agon* means side, so a seven-sided figure is a:

18. Draw a full turn of this rectangle.

19. Draw in the missing axes of symmetry in this square.

20. Plot the points X(2, B), Y(4, D) and Z(5, A). Name the shape formed when X, Y and Z are joined.

Statistics and Probability

21. What is the total mass of the three (A, B, C) objects?

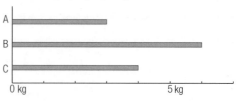

22. If I toss two coins, what are the possible outcomes?

How is a volcano formed?

The earth is made up of three layers: the crust, the mantle and the core. The outer layer, called the crust, is between 16 and 40 kilometres thick. It floats on a thicker layer known as the mantle, which is 2895 kilometres thick. The core, which is 3475 kilometres thick, is surrounded by the mantle. The innermost part is solid (the inner core) while the outer part is liquid (the outer core). The earth's core contains materials made up of atoms, which send out flying particles or rays. These are called radioactive materials and the particles or rays are called radiation. When these particles are sent out a lot of energy is released and this causes the earth's core to reach a temperature of approximately 20 000 degrees Celsius. The heat from the core passes into the mantle, which can reach temperatures of around 10 000 degrees Celsius. In some parts of the mantle the heat builds up to such an extent that it melts some of the rock material of the lower crust. Geologists call the melted rock magma.

Sometimes the pressure in the magma chamber builds up so much that it finds a weak area in the crust and forces its way to the surface of the earth. Once the magma reaches the surface it is called lava. The lava then builds up on the surface of the earth, where it slowly cools and turns into solid rock.

Reading and Comprehension

1. A scientist who studies the earth is a

   _____ .

2. What is the difference between lava and magma?

   _____

3. The core of the earth is
   (a) 16 km below the surface.
   (b) 40 km below the surface.
   (c) 2895 km below the surface.
   (d) between 2911 and 2935 km below the surface.

4. The extreme heat of the core is caused by
   (a) radioactive materials.   (b) radiation.
   (c) Celsius.   (d) atoms.

5. Number these statements in order (1–4).
   (a) Magma forces its way through cracks towards the surface.
   (b) Some magma reaches the surface.
   (c) Parts of the mantle become extremely hot.
   (d) Lower parts of the crust become so hot that the rock melts.

Spelling and Vocabulary

Rewrite the misspelt words.

6. The plain flew at high altitude. _____

7. He fell of his bike. _____

Circle the word that has the nearest meaning to the underlined word.

8. Please do not be rude.
   (a) clever   (b) late
   (c) careless   (d) bad mannered

9. This pane of glass is smooth.
   (a) cracked   (b) clear
   (c) without lumps   (d) thick

Circle the correct word in brackets.

10. He (dyed, died) from a gun shot wound.

11. You look (pail, pale) after that frightening experience.

12. The lounge (sweet, suite) needs to be cleaned.

Grammar and Punctuation

13. Give the plural form of these **nouns**.

    duck _____   loaf _____

    roof _____   child _____

    ox _____

14. Punctuate and capitalise this sentence.

    cant you come on saturday

    _____

Number and Algebra

1.

+	8	5	6	7	2	74
3						

2.

−	16	11	18	15	12	35
9						

3.

×	5	2	7	3	9	11
7						

4. Write five thousand and eighty-seven as a numeral.

5. Continue the pattern:

2543, 3543, [   ] , [   ]

6. Draw and colour 4 out of nine.

7. Paul bought two sandwiches each costing 50 cents, a juice for 30 cents and an apple for 25 cents. How much change did he get from $3.00?

8. $\frac{7}{10}$ equals **0.**

9. Round 6028 off to the nearest hundred.

10. I have 2 kg sugar, 1 kg flour, 500 g rice, a 200 g jar of honey and 500 g of butter. What is the total?

Measurement and Geometry

11. In a quarter of an hour it will be 6:05. What is the time now?

12. Correct this statement: My classmate Brian has a mass of 48 g.

13. Find the perimeter of this rectangle in centimetres.

19 cm

40 cm

14. 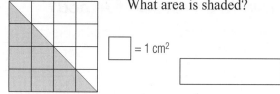 What area is shaded?

[ ] = 1 cm²

15. 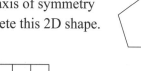 How much less than 1 L is the total volume?

500 mL   400 mL

16. Today was very hot. What was the temperature? 14 °C or 34 °C

17. I have 4 right angles, 2 diagonals and 4 axes of symmetry. What am I?

18. Draw a reflex angle.

19. Use the axis of symmetry to complete this 2D shape.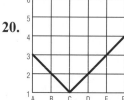

20. 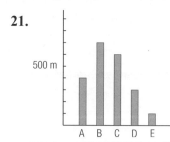 Name the fourth point to make this shape a rectangle.

Statistics and Probability

21. This graph shows the distance from X to each of these points. Which pairs add up to 1 kilometre?

500 m

A B C D E

22. y = yellow, r = red. Label the remainder of the spinner so that it is most likely to land on yellow.

Life in the sea

One of the most important forms of life in Antarctica are tiny animals known as krill. These are similar to prawns, though smaller. In summer they can be found in huge swarms in many parts of the Antarctic Ocean. Krill are important because they in turn become the food for many other sea creatures—fish, birds, seals and whales.

These krill are the staple diet for the largest animal in the world, the blue whale. This whale can grow to a length of 30 metres and weigh up to 180 tonnes. An adult blue whale is capable of eating four tonnes of krill in a day. It catches the krill by passing sea water through thousands of baleen (or bony plates) in its mouth which act like a sieve. Other baleen whales are the fin, minke, humpback, sei and southern right whales. The blue whale is by far the largest.

Some whale species have teeth and feed on larger creatures. For example, sperm whales eat squid, and killer whales will feed on penguins, seals, fish and other whales.

Southern Hemisphere whales spend the summer in Antarctic waters near the edge of the pack-ice, feeding and increasing their body weight enormously so that they have great reserves of blubber to give them energy for the rest of the year. In autumn they move north into subtropical waters to give birth to their young.

Reading and Comprehension

1. Name the largest animal in the world.

   _____

2. What name is given to a big group of krill?

   _____

3. Krill are members of the family of
   (a) whales.   (b) fish.
   (c) prawns.   (d) crabs.

4. Whales without teeth get their food by
   (a) swallowing it in one gulp.
   (b) sieving the food from the water.
   (c) eating soft food like squid.
   (d) not eating much during winter.

5. Match these activities with the season.
   (a) feeding up   (1) autumn
   (b) migrating north   (2) spring
   (c) giving birth   (3) summer
   (d) returning south   (4) autumn

Spelling and Vocabulary

Rewrite the misspelt words.

6. He bought his bike to school.

   _____

7. His throat is saw.

   _____

Circle the word that has the nearest meaning to the underlined word.

8. The junior classes have sport today.
   (a) younger   (b) new
   (c) best   (d) clever

9. The donkey was beaten by his cruel owner.
   (a) hit   (b) fed
   (c) scolded   (d) ridden

Circle the correct word in brackets.

10. We (herd, heard) the bell ring.

11. I was (weak, week) after my long illness.

12. This is not a good (place, palace) to hide.

Grammar and Punctuation

13. Change these plural **pronouns** to singular form.

   We will be going to our school with them.

   _____

14. Punctuate and capitalise this sentence.

   he dived into the cool clear water

   _____

Number and Algebra

1. Follow this addition path.

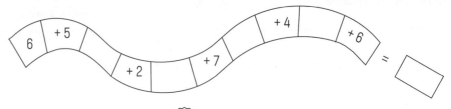

2. Work your way down these subtraction ladders.

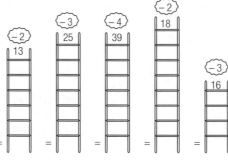

3. Complete the missing numbers in these statements.
   (a) $3 \times 6 =$ ____, $6 \times 3 =$ ____, ____ $\div 6 = 3$, ____ $\div 3 = 6$
   (b) If $5 \times 7 = 35$ then $7 \times 5 =$ ____, $35 \div 7 =$ ____, and $35 \div 5 =$ ____
   (c) $4 \times 0 =$ ____, $0 \times 4 =$ ____ and $0 \div 4 =$ ____
   (d) $8 \times 8 =$ ____, $64 \div 8 =$ ____, and eight squared is equal to ____

4. Arrange the digits 4, 2, 7 and 3 so that the four has the value of 4 tens, the seven means 7000, the two means two ones and the three is three hundreds.

5. Jemma was counting in 5s. Go on in this series: 570, 575, ▢ , ▢ , ▢

6.  What fraction of this grid has been shaded?

7. What is the total of these coins?

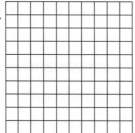

8. Shade in 0.52 of this grid.

9. If I round off 7642 to the nearest hundred, my answer is:
   (a) 7700   (b) 7600   (c) 8000   (d) 7000

10. What is the total mass of all these objects?
    4 kg   750 g   75 g   1500 g

Measurement and Geometry

11. Show twenty to eight on these clocks. 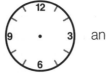 and

12. A block of wood is balanced on a scale by 3 one hundred gram, two 50 g
and 4 twenty gram masses. The block weighs:

13.

    (a) Convert all these measurements to centimetres.

    (b) Calculate the perimeter of the shape.

14.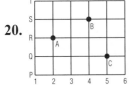

    What area of this grid is covered
by the shaded triangle?

15. I have a $\frac{1}{2}$ litre of juice and add 400 mL of water.
How much less than one litre will I have?

16. At 8 am the temperature was 15 °C. By midday it rose by 8°.
By late afternoon it had fallen back by 4°. The temperature then was:

17. Which of these statements about rectangles is not true?
    (a) Rectangles are very thin.   (c) All rectangles have a breadth.
    (b) The long side of a rectangle is the length.

18. Name these angles.

    (a)   (b)
    (c)   (d)

19. Which of these lines are not
axes of symmetry?

20. 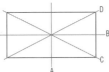 B is at (4, Q), (S, 4), (5, N) or (4, S).

    Choose the correct one.

Statistics and Probability

21. Plot this tally of pet fish
on this bar graph.

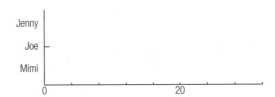

22. In rolling two dice, what are all the possible outcomes?

Radio News

Although most people say they get their news from television, when some event is occurring, people usually first turn on the radio for information. This is so for several reasons: radio is more accessible than the other media; its news bulletins are more frequent; radio news journalists are usually able to get to the scene of an event more quickly and get the news onto the airwaves sooner; and radio can involve its listeners in the news more easily. Radio is, then, a valuable news source.

Radio is more accessible for a number of reasons. One is that every home, almost every car and a large number of public places have one. This means that it is easy to find a radio and turn it on. Another is that some radios are so small it is possible to carry one in a pocket and listen to it whenever you want. Finally, you can listen to the radio while you do other things. It does not matter if you are in bed or at the beach, driving a car or camping in the country, walking around the street or working in the backyard, radio news is accessible. While newspaper and television channels usually have only one main edition each day, radio news programs broadcast frequently. Radio stations have a news bulletin at least every hour. This means that radio can report events as they happen and update the reports as more information is gathered.

Radio can be first with the news because radio journalists do not have to set up the equipment that television journalists need. This means radio journalists can quickly arrive at an event with just their smartphone and laptop or iPad. Unlike in the other two media, radio journalists can go to air quickly, simply by telephoning their station or by using a small radio handset, much like a walkie-talkie.

Radio news can involve listeners more effectively than the other media. It can seek opinions, questions, comments and further information through talkback radio. It can also abandon all its other programs to concentrate on an important story and to provide a community service. A good example is the way radio news responded to the Ash Wednesday bushfires in 1983.

In February 1983, bushfires erupted across southern Australia from Adelaide to Melbourne. Flames roared through bushland, across farms and through towns to the edges of the big cities, destroying all before them. Thousands of farm and native animals were burnt to death. People fleeing the fires huddled together in halls, schools and on the beaches. Seventy-two people died. Many more became separated from friends and family.

It was one of the worst natural disasters in Australia's history. People's responses were demonstrations of the finest human qualities.

As the wind carried ashes from the fires over the city, people turned to their radios for information about the extent of the fires and the damage, the safety of friends and relatives, and where it was safe to go. Radio stations, especially 3AW in Melbourne, sent journalists to the main fire areas. Nobody who heard journalist Murray Nicoll describe the fires in Adelaide will forget hearing him say, "At the moment I'm watching my house burn down. I'm sitting out on the road in front of my own house where I've lived for 15 or 14 years and it's going down in front of me. The roof is falling in. It's in flames and there's nothing I can do about it. Absolutely nothing ... The flames are in the roof ... It's just beyond belief. My own house! Everything around is black. There are fires burning all around me."

Murray Nicoll believed he would die that day. As he said, "I've been in some bad fires but this was unbelievable. I thought if we're going to die, people are going to hear about it so I turned on the two-way radio handset and started broadcasting. After all, I thought, that's my job." As well as informing people about the extent of the fires and the damage they caused, radio news ran appeals to collect food, clothing, blankets and other necessary items for people who had suffered losses. It helped keep traffic out of dangerous areas, put people in touch with each other and appealed for volunteers to fight the fires. This was radio news at its best.

Reading and Comprehension

1. What equipment do radio journalists need?

   _____

2. How frequently are radio news reports broadcast?

   _____

3. Which of the following doesn't make radio news more accessible?

   (a) You can do other things and still listen to the radio.

   (b) Radios are very common.

   (c) Radios are cheap.

   (d) Radios are quite small.

4. The Ash Wednesday bushfires in 1983 were spread across

   (a) Melbourne.

   (b) Adelaide.

   (c) Melbourne and Adelaide.

   (d) southern Australia.

5. Number these sentences in order (1–4).

   (a) Murray reported that his house was on fire.

   (b) He thought that he would die that day.

   (c) Murray Nicoll turned on his two-way radio and began to broadcast.

   (d) Everything around him was black. Fires were all around him.

Spelling and Vocabulary

Rewrite the misspelt words.

6. Seventy-two people died. Many more became seperated from friends and family.

   _____

   _____

   _____

   _____

7. Flames roared threw bushland, across farms and though towns to the edges of the big cities, destroying all befor them.

   _____

   _____

   _____

Circle the word that has the nearest meaning to the underlined word.

8. It can seek opinions, comments and further information through talkback radio.
   (a) people's views   (b) support
   (c) better ratings   (d) people's participation

9. It was one of the worst natural disasters in Australia's history.
   (a) caused by humans
   (b) caused by industries
   (c) not caused by people
   (d) happens easily

Circle the correct word in brackets.

10. People are going to (here, hear) about this.

11. This is (so, sew) for several reasons.

12. (Its, It's) news bulletins are more frequent.

Grammar and Punctuation

13. Write the **plural** form of these words.

    news _____   radio _____

    listener _____   flame _____

    roof _____   program _____

    journalist _____

14. Rewrite this sentence with correct punctuation and capitalisation.

    i heard him say at the moment im watching my house burn down

    _____

    _____

    _____

Number and Algebra

1.

+	5	6	8	7	1	39
0						

2.

−	13	15	12	9	14	51
7						

3.

÷	63	27	9	81	54	108
9						

4. Write the numeral for 5000 + 400 + 60 + 7.

5. Write the first five even numbers.

☐ , ☐ , ☐ , ☐ , ☐

6. Which is greater, 45 out of 100 or $\frac{46}{100}$?

7. What change do I get from $10 after buying 3 books each costing $1.50?

8. Write seventy-four per cent in the shortened form.

9. Round 4497 off to the nearest thousand.

10. 246 men and 309 women attended the concert. If each paid $2, how much was collected?

Measurement and Geometry

11. Write 3:10 am in analogue form.

12. Circle the masses greater than l kg.

792 g   1056 g   2875 g   96 g

13. Write 4 metres 28 centimetres in decimal form.

14. What is the area of this shape?

☐ square units

15. How many cubic centimetres would fit in a box 3 cm long, 2 cm wide and 2 cm deep?

16. The temperature was 28 °C. Overnight it fell by 9°. What was the new temperature?

17. When a sphere is cut in cross-section, the shape formed by the cut is a:

18. Draw in BC so that ∠ABC is a right angle.

19. Complete this shape based on the line of symmetry.

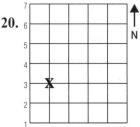

20. From the start X go north 2 units and east 3 units. Give the coordinates of that point.

Statistics and Probability

21. If 🐟 is used to represent 10 fish, show these children's catches on the graph: Paul 15, Mary 20, Thomas 25

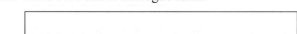

Paul

Mary

Thomas

22. If I toss a coin 50 times, what result would you expect?

heads   tails

Waste disposal

The common methods of waste disposal are burial in landfill tips, incineration and storage. There are problems associated with all of these methods. Firstly, space for landfill tips is limited. If chemicals are stored, they can leak, and no one is certain about the effect of chemicals being released into the atmosphere after they are incinerated, or what is left in the ashes.

Some products take many years to decompose. These include those made of plastics, heavy metals and toxic materials. Most of us do not realise that we use these products nearly every day in some form. How often do we drink from plastic straws or use batteries that contain the deadly metal, mercury?

Australia has no efficient way of disposing of extremely toxic chemicals, so they are shipped overseas for incineration. Debate is continuing over constructing an incinerator in Australia. Some people consider incinerators unsafe while others think there is no alternative.

Most toxic chemicals are buried in concrete-lined underground cells. In some areas the concrete has cracked, releasing the chemicals into the surrounding soil. Once contaminated, the soil is unfit for use.

Reading and Comprehension

1. Does Australia have its own toxic chemical incinerator? _____

2. In your own words explain the meaning of the word *decompose*. _____
_____

3. How does Australia dispose of its toxic chemicals?
   (a) We ship them overseas for burial.
   (b) We transport them to other countries to be burnt.
   (c) We bury them here in Australia.
   (d) We don't use toxic materials.

4. In which of these would you find mercury?
   (a) remote control for a TV
   (b) Walkman radio
   (c) battery-operated toys
   (d) camera flash unit

5. Match the following waste item with the problem it can cause.

   (a) plastic   (1) atmospheric pollution
   (b) toxic chemicals   (2) remain in people's bodies
   (c) heavy metals   (3) many years to decompose
   (d) burnt chemicals   (4) contaminate soil when they leak out

Spelling and Vocabulary

Rewrite the misspelt words.

6. It's allmost five o'clock. _____

7. Use your nife and fork correctly. _____

Circle the word that has the nearest meaning to the underlined word.

8. The engine would not <u>operate</u>.
   (a) go   (b) stop
   (c) turn   (d) go faster

9. He <u>swerved</u> to miss the hole.
   (a) braked   (b) accelerated
   (c) slowed down   (d) turned sharply

Circle the correct word in brackets.

10. Have they (sung, sang) together?
11. Ina went to choir (practice, practise).
12. Mum has a gold (brooch, broach).

Grammar and Punctuation

13. Write the plurals of these **nouns**.

   tooth _____ woman _____

   mouse _____ goose _____

   foot _____

14. Punctuate and capitalise this sentence.

   did you learn about asia africa europe and australia last year

   _____
   _____

Number and Algebra

1.

+	5	6	3	8	9	32
4						

2.

−	9	12	14	1	8	53
0						

3.

×	2	8	3	7	4	11
9						

4. Expand 3852. ____ + ____ + ____ + ____

5. Write the next four odd numbers:

17, _____ , _____ , _____ ,

6. Shade $\frac{4}{10}$ of the shape.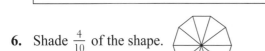

7. Pencils are 25c each. How many can I buy for $2.00? _____

8. $0.65 = \dfrac{\boxed{}}{100} = \boxed{}$ %

9. 1437 rounded off to the nearest hundred is 1500. True or false? _____

10. From her bank account of $89.15, Tina withdrew $17.50. How much is her balance now? _____

Measurement and Geometry

11. Twenty to five in the afternoon is

_____ am / pm in digital form.

12. Write six hundred and forty grams in shortened form. _____

13. Circle the greater distance:
6.4 metres   OR   6 metres 4 centimetres

14. Circle which unit of area is best to measure:
(a) the floor   (cm² / m²)
(b) your notebook   (cm² / m²)
(c) a postage stamp   (cm² / m²)
(d) the lawn   (cm² / m²)

15. 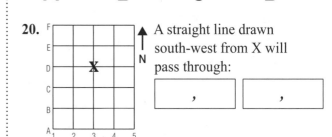 How many cubic centimetres are needed to make this shape? _____

16. The thermometer read 18 °C. Sam plunged it in hot water and it rose by 27° to read: _____

17. A cone has (1 / 2 / many) vertices. _____

18. Draw a straight angle.

19. Draw in the line of symmetry in these letters.

A   B   C   D

20. A straight line drawn south-west from X will pass through: _____ , _____

Statistics and Probability

21. ⌂ is used to represent 10 houses.

Morgan St ⌂ ⌂ ⌂
Rode Rd ⌂ ⌂ ⌂
Colourful Ct ⌂ ⌂ ⌂ ⌂ ⌂

What is the total number of houses in all 3 streets? _____

22. There are 25 marbles in a bag, 20 red and 5 blue. What colour marble is most likely to be drawn from the bag? _____

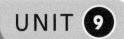

Introducing the camel

One interesting animal first arrived in Australia in 1849: the camel. This was the one-humped camel, also called the dromedary (not to be confused with its two-humped cousin, the Bactrian camel).

The dromedary is native to the Middle East and mainland Asia, whose desert peoples have domesticated and used the camel for about 5000 years. The camel's strength is used for transport and farming; its meat and milk for food; its fur and skin for clothing and shelter.

Camels are especially suited to desert life, for several reasons. They can go without water for days, even weeks. Their mouths are tough enough to chew the thorniest shrub. But they can go for many days without food, because they carry a built-in food supply: their humps, where fat is stored to provide energy in lean times.

Because camels can drink huge amounts of water, people once thought they must be able to store water in their humps. Not so, say the scientists; they just replace what their system has lost.

Camels have thick eyebrows and lashes to shelter their eyes from sun and sand. Lips, ears and nostrils can shut tight to keep out sand and dust.

Camels have thick, broad pads on each foot that help them to run or walk on sand, where hard-hoofed animals would sink at every step.

The camel's ability to survive without water in hot, dry conditions, and to travel long distances carrying people and goods, has given it the name 'ship of the desert'.

Reading and Comprehension

1. A two-humped camel is called a
    _____ camel.

2. Camels can be milked. True or false?

3. Camels' humps are used to
    (a) store water.
    (b) help them digest food.
    (c) enable them to chew thorny bushes.
    (d) store food as fat.

4. Camels have thick, wide feet so that they can
    (a) run fast.
    (b) survive in the desert.
    (c) travel long distances.
    (d) walk or run on soft surfaces.

5. Number these statements in order (1–4).
    (a) Scientists say that this is not true.
    (b) Camels can drink a lot of water.
    (c) Camels replace lost water in their bodies.
    (d) Some say camels store water in their humps.

Spelling and Vocabulary

Rewrite the misspelt words.

6. It is nearly a mounth till we go away.

    _____

7. Offten we have takeaway meals.

    _____

Circle the word that has the nearest meaning to the underlined word.

8. Take hold of the <u>thick</u> end of the bat.
    (a) smooth   (b) wide
    (c) heavy   (d) thin

9. <u>Bind</u> his hands and feet together.
    (a) tie   (b) hold
    (c) keep   (d) gather

Circle the correct word in brackets.

10. Mike is the (heir, air) to the family fortune.

11. (Coarse, Course) cloth makes me itchy.

12. There is a strong (current, currant) in this stream.

Grammar and Punctuation

13. Choose the correct **pronoun**.

    (I, my, me, mine) will be late if (I, my, me, mine) bus doesn't come soon.

14. Punctuate and capitalise this sentence.

    it is a turtle replied jim

    _____

Number and Algebra

1.

+	7	6	1	0	8	85
2						

2.

−	7	14	5	9	12	33
5						

3.

÷	36	6	42	54	24	48
6						

4. What is 7000 + 600 + 9? ☐

5. Count on from 680 in 10s.

☐ , ☐ , ☐ , ☐

6. Write the fraction for the part that is coloured.

☐

7. Rulers cost 95c each. How many can I buy for $5? ☐

8. **0.** ☐ = $\frac{37}{100}$ = ☐ %

9. Circle the numbers which will round off to 6000:

6972, 5874, 5099, 6079.

10. Ice cream is $4.96 for 4 litres. How much will 6 litres cost? ☐

Measurement and Geometry

11. 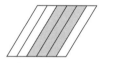 is the same as ☐ **:** ☐ am.

12. Is a pencil (more / less) than 100 grams? ☐

13.

5.12 m

3.46 m

Calculate the perimeter. ☐

14.  What area has been shaded? ☐

15. I made a shape 8 cm long, 2 cm wide and 1 cm high. How many cubic centimetre blocks did I use? ☐

16. What is the temperature shown on this Celsius thermometer?

40°

20°

☐

17. Circle the shape that is most easily stacked:

sphere   cone   cylinder

18. An acute angle is greater than or less than a right angle? ☐

19. This rectangle ▭ has 2 lines of symmetry.

This rectangle ▭ is bigger, so it has more lines of symmetry. True or false? ☐

20.

If the points (B, 5), (C, 4) and (D, 3) are joined, what shape will be formed? ☐

Statistics and Probability

21. Use the symbol $ to represent 5 dollars. Show these amounts:

$20 ☐ $25 ☐

$50 ☐ $7.50 ☐

22. Fill a jar with 10 red and 10 blue counters. How many counters must be drawn before you will be certain to have two of a colour? ☐

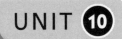

Making your own kite

Kites come in many shapes and sizes. They can be constructed from a large variety of materials, from the simplest, such as paper or cloth, to the most advanced, such as carbon fibre and tear-proof sailsheet.

Kites can be quite easy to make. As with most things, it is best to master the simplest kites first, before you advance to state-of-the-art kite building.

To build your kite you will need a few supplies. For the frame you will need timber. Hobby shops and timber yards are the best sources for light timbers such as bamboo, pine and Australian mountain ash. The timber should be round. Ask for dowel; they'll know what you need. Garden shops are a good source for bamboo. For the covering skin you can use paper, plastic or cloth. Some of these materials will tear in strong winds, so you will need some reinforcing tape.

The beauty of these materials is that they can be easily decorated with paint, drawings and pictures. To fly the kite you will also need a good length of string.

Much of this material can be found in the rubbish bin. Constructed from recycled materials and powered by the wind, your kite will be the ultimate in environmentally sound machines!

Reading and Comprehension

1. Name two modern materials used to make state-of-the-art kites.

   _____

2. What name is given to round timber?

   _____

3. If you wish to use Australian mountain ash for your frame, the best source would be
   (a) timber suppliers.   (b) hobby shops.
   (c) garden shops.   (d) a dowel manufacturer.

4. After building the kite frame, the next step is to
   (a) find a good length of string.
   (b) use tape to reinforce your kite.
   (c) cover the frame with paper.
   (d) decorate your kite.

5. Number these directions about kite construction in order (1–4).
   (a) Cover your frame.
   (b) Fly your finished kite.
   (c) Decorate the kite.
   (d) Make the frame.

Spelling and Vocabulary

Rewrite the misspelt words.

6. Her happyness is shown on her face. _____

7. My freind Mick is a good footballer. _____

Circle the word that has the nearest meaning to the underlined word.

8. It was a peculiar sight.
   (a) wonderful   (b) strange
   (c) familiar   (d) terrible

9. She was very nervous.
   (a) afraid   (b) fast
   (c) dangerous   (d) still

Circle the correct word in brackets.

10. Mum was (dyeing, dying) my T-shirt.

11. The soldier went (fourth, forth) into battle.

12. He (fought, fort) bravely.

Grammar and Punctuation

13. Write a sentence with the word *damage* used as a **noun**.

    _____

14. Punctuate and capitalise this sentence.

    it isnt too late he replied

    _____

    _____

Number and Algebra

1.

+	9	7	0	4	3	46
5						

2.

−	8	14	6	10	12	31
6						

3.

×	8	7	1	9	6	17
1						

4. Expand 4407.

[+   +   ]

5. Count backwards in hundreds from 4020.

[   ] , [   ] , [   ]

6. $\frac{18}{18}$ or 18 out of 18 children watch TV. Does this mean no / all children watch TV?

7. We spent $15 on meat, $27 on groceries and $9 on pastries. Will a $50 note be enough? Yes or no?

8. I've used 54% of my money. What percentage do I have left?

9. Round 2500 off to the nearest thousand.

10. Our car uses 10 litres of petrol every 100 kilometres. In 790 kilometres it will use:

Measurement and Geometry

11. Show 11:45 on this clock face.

12. A family meat pie has a mass of 950 g. How much less than 1 kg is this?

13. 7.08 m is equal to:

7 [   ] and [   ] centimetres

14. Write one hundred and forty-five square centimetres in shortened form.

15. 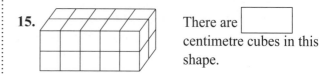 There are [   ] centimetre cubes in this shape.

16. Write forty-four degrees Celsius in shortened form.

17.  Draw in the line of cross-section that will give this cone a triangular shape when cut.

18. An obtuse angle is [   ] than a right angle but less than a [   ] angle.

19. Complete this shape using the two lines of symmetry.

20. 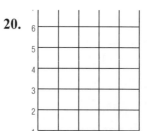 Name the angle formed at C when these points are plotted and joined: (B, 4), (C, 1) and (E, 6).

Statistics and Probability

21. For every 8 books that he was able to read, Sunin was given a merit sticker. How many stickers will he receive for this tally of books?
𝍥 𝍥 𝍥 𝍥 𝍥 𝍥 𝍥

22. I put 6 green, 2 red and 1 yellow bead into a bag. If I draw them out one at a time, which colour is least likely to be drawn first of all?

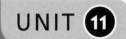
Soil erosion

Soil erosion is the natural process in which soil is carried away by water and wind and deposited somewhere else, usually at the bottom of the ocean. Usually, the process of erosion is balanced by the processes that build the soil up. Scientists estimate that the natural process of soil formation can take from 100 to 2500 years to produce about 2.5 cm of topsoil.

Plants and trees hold the topsoil in place. When they are removed, the topsoil is exposed and easily washed away by rain, or blown away by the wind. The wrong use of technology and poor land management can destroy soil that took millions of years to develop, in just 10 years.

The natural process of erosion has increased since humans began to plough the soil for crops and clear the land to feed grazing animals. Bad land management practices, such as ploughing and clearing steep slopes, using too much irrigation and having too many animals grazing on pastures, help to remove vegetation and leave the soil open to the effects of wind and rain. Perhaps the most destructive practice is the removal of forest. At present, we remove 15 million hectares of forest each year, and the world loses approximately 80 billion tonnes of soil each year.

Reading and Comprehension

1. Where does eroded soil usually end up?

   _____

2. How much topsoil is eroded each year?

   _____

3. Which of the following practices increase(s) erosion?
   (a) clearing sloping land
   (b) too much irrigation
   (c) overgrazing
   (d) all of the above

4. What holds topsoil in place?
   (a) wind   (b) rain
   (c) plants   (d) animals

5. Number these statements in order (1–4).
   (a) Plants and trees hold the topsoil in place.
   (b) Soil build-up is a natural process.
   (c) Soil erosion can take place quite quickly.
   (d) Forming soil takes hundreds, perhaps thousands of years.

Spelling and Vocabulary

Rewrite the misspelt words.

6. I'll meet you on Wenesday. _____

7. My Dad will be fourty in January. _____

Circle the word that has the nearest meaning to the underlined word.

8. He was a <u>bold</u> adventurer.
   (a) brave   (b) old
   (c) strong   (d) good

9. The area was covered in <u>litter</u>.
   (a) insects   (b) leaves
   (c) flowers   (d) rubbish

Circle the correct word in brackets.

10. Lu gave out a cry of (pain, pane).

11. Did you hear that low (groan, grown)?

12. I lost the (hole, whole) purse of money.

Grammar and Punctuation

13. Write a sentence with the word *damage* used as a **verb**.

    _____

    _____

    _____

14. Punctuate and capitalise this sentence.

    is this a turtle asked sean

    _____

    _____

Number and Algebra

1.

+	5	6	4	7	1	88
6						

2.

−	9	17	8	14	16	35
8						

3.

÷	21	15	3	9	27	36
3						

4. 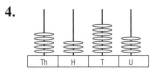 Write the number shown on the abacus.

5. What number is a hundred more than 2987?

6. Circle the greater fraction: $\frac{40}{100}$ or $\frac{63}{100}$

7 From $20, Jacinta spent $1.89 on lollies, $4.95 on entertainment and $3.75 on magazines. How much has she left?

8 Choose the equivalents to 0.47

$\frac{53}{100}$ 0.53   47% $\frac{15}{100}$ $\frac{47}{100}$

9. 61 586 rounded off to the nearest thousand is:

10 Soft drink is 57c a can. What will a carton of 30 cans cost?

Measurement and Geometry

11. It is now 11:56 am. What will the time be in a quarter of an hour?

12. Cakes of soap have a mass of 125 g. There are [ ] cakes of soap in 1 kg.

13. 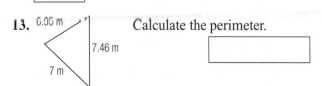 Calculate the perimeter.

0.05 m
7.46 m
7 m

14. A square with a side of 1 metre has an area of 1 m² / 4 m.

15. Draw a rectangular prism that has a volume of 4 cm³.

16. What's the difference between 16 °C and 33 °C?

17. Name the 3D shape that has no edges, no vertices and no flat faces.

18. If the angle is more than a straight angle, it is called a [ ] angle.

19. Complete this symmetrical pattern of lines.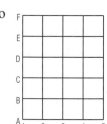

20. Name the other point needed to make the shape into a square.
(3, A), (1, C), (3, E) and [ ]

Statistics and Probability

21. Use the key [car] = 10 cars to record this data on the picture graph. Monday 25 cars, Tuesday 20, Wednesday 30, Thursday 15, Friday 35

M
T
W
T
F

22. If I placed 3 blue, 3 red and 4 green counters in a bag and then made 100 drawings from the bag, what results would you expect?

blue drawn [ ] times, green [ ] times and red [ ] times

Landfills

At no time in history have humans produced so much waste. Ours is a throw-away society. No matter which area is examined it is found that, for health, safety, advertising, presentation or other reasons, we produce more waste. This means our landfills are being used up at an unprecedented rate because of this increasing volume of waste.

Many people consider landfills to be time bombs waiting to explode because of the vast quantity of chemicals or gases that leach from them as the waste contained in them begins to degrade or rot away.

The gas methane, given off by rotting waste, can be most dangerous, but it can be used. If a series of pipes is laid through the landfill, the gas can be collected. This gas can then be burnt in a controlled way and used to generate electricity, which can be fed into the grid and help supply electricity for consumers.

With further research more ideas could be implemented. Landfills are a problem but humanity's wealth of ideas and technology can, and will, surely make use of people's waste.

Reading and Comprehension

1. What leaches from landfills?

   _____

2. Name the landfill gas used to generate electricity.

   _____

3. From this text, what is the author's opinion of landfills?
   (a) They are good.
   (b) They are bad.
   (c) We need more landfills to generate more electricity.
   (d) Landfills are necessary. They have problems but some problems can be solved.

4. We are filling up our landfills at a greater rate because
   (a) there are fewer landfills.
   (b) there are more landfills.
   (c) we create more waste.
   (d) populations have grown.

5. Number these statements in order (1–4).
   (a) Electricity is available for consumers.
   (b) Methane is burnt.
   (c) The heat from burning generates electricity.
   (d) Rotting materials give off a gas.

Spelling and Vocabulary

Rewrite the misspelt words.

6. He causes too much truble. _____

7. My woolen jumper is too hot in September.

   _____

Circle the word that has the nearest meaning to the underlined word.

8. I'm <u>positive</u> he's the one.
   (a) sure   (b) pleased
   (c) hoping   (d) lucky

9. The clock chimes at <u>noon</u>.
   (a) play time   (b) midnight
   (c) home time   (d) midday

Circle the correct word in brackets.

10. (Its, It's) time to get up.

11. You are so (idle, idol).

12. (Weave, We've) been away on holidays.

Grammar and Punctuation

13. Is the word underlined a **verb** or a **noun** in this sentence?

    <u>Light</u> the lamp so we can see. _____

14. Punctuate and capitalise this sentence.

    he did it on purpose i replied

    _____

Number and Algebra

1.

+	2	7	4	8	6	29
8						

2.

−	12	10	9	13	11	38
4						

3.

×	7	1	9	3	5	12
8						

4. Show 5082 on this abacus.

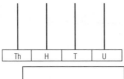

5. Write the number 10 less than 3607.

6. Arrange these fractions from smallest to largest:

$$\frac{33}{100} \quad \frac{30}{100} \quad \frac{13}{100}$$

7. I had $100 and I spent it all. $55.60 on petrol, $26.90 on food and the rest on entertainment. How much did I spend on entertainment?

8. Which is greater, 8% or 80%?

9. 40 498 rounds off to [   ] when taken to the nearest thousand.

10. What is the difference between 836 and 578?

Measurement and Geometry

11. It's now 11:35 pm. In half an hour it will be:

12. What is the total mass of these three items?

13. 491 cm = [   ] m

14. A rectangle has an area of 12 cm². If it is 4 cm long, how wide is it?

15. A cube with each side of 1 cm has a volume of:

16. Water freezes at [   ] °C and boils at [   ] °C.

17. Match the name of the 3D shape to what happens when it is rolled.

Sphere   (a) rolls round in a circle
Cone   (b) rolls in a straight line
Cylinder   (c) rolls in any direction

18. Link the type to the angle.

Acute   Right   Obtuse   Straight   Reflex

19. Draw in the lines of symmetry for each:

20. Plot the points X(B,1) and Y(F,4). If a line is drawn from X to Y the line is pointing in which direction?

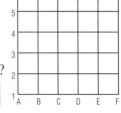

Statistics and Probability

21. If represents 20 fish, how many fish did Pete catch on these days?

Monday   = [   ]

Wednesday   = [   ]

Friday      = [   ]

Saturday      = [   ]

22. Tina tossed a 20 cent coin ten times and recorded ten heads. Is this possible?

The first spider

A princess called Arachne lived in Greece some years before 1000 BC. She was a weaver of exquisite tapestries. Her creations hung in her father's palace. The proud king would boast: "Her genius is a gift from the goddess Athena."

"No, not even Athena, our patron goddess of weaving, can match our daughter," the queen would add.

Arachne loved to hear such compliments, while pretending to be unworthy of them. But one day, as she was hanging one of her tapestries in Athena's temple, she was so overpowered by the beauty of her work that she exclaimed, "Not even you, Athena, can better this!"

High above on Mount Olympus, Athena heard. She'd never been envious of a mortal, but this boast pierced her like a poisoned arrow. Athena appeared like a bolt of lightning before the startled Arachne. "How dare you challenge me!" she roared in anger. Arachne trembled, terrified. Should she prostrate herself, or run for her life? Before she could do anything, 2 black squares of cloth and a pile of coloured threads materialised at her feet.

"I accept your challenge!" Athena thundered. "Take as much thread as you need."

Arachne's fear vanished; her life was not in danger. Instead, the goddess of weaving wanted to pit her skill against Arachne's. "Each of us will tell a story about the lives of the gods, within these golden borders," Athena said as she plucked two identical golden threads from the air. "When the tapestries are completed, let the gods decide which of us is the greatest weaver."

Reading and Comprehension

1. How long ago did this story take place?

   _____

2. In which country is Mount Olympus? _____

3. Athena appeared before Arachne because
   (a) Arachne had challenged her.
   (b) Athena was envious of Arachne's boast.
   (c) Arachne struck Athena with a poisoned arrow.
   (d) Athena wanted to see Arachne's tapestry.

4. Athena wanted to
   (a) destroy Arachne.
   (b) challenge Arachne.
   (c) tell Arachne about the lives of the gods.
   (d) bring Arachne before the other gods.

5. Number these sentences in order (1–4).
   (a) The gods would decide who was the best weaver.
   (b) Arachne was very proud of her work.
   (c) The two would each create a tapestry.
   (d) Athena was angry at Arachne's boasting.

Spelling and Vocabulary

Rewrite the misspelt words.

6. I'll have the smaller peace please. _____

7. Lisa writes a nice pome. _____

Circle the word that has the nearest meaning to the underlined word.

8. I can do that with ease.
   (a) some help   (b) no delay
   (c) no trouble   (d) pride

9. He deserved his punishment.
   (a) reward   (b) prize
   (c) retribution   (d) promise

Circle the correct word in brackets.

10. Thou shalt not (steal, steel).

11. My coat is (worn, warn) out.

12. (Where's, Wears) the soap?

Grammar and Punctuation

13. Is the word *collar* used as a **noun** or a **verb** here?
    Collar the dog before it
    jumps up on our visitor. _____

14. Punctuate and capitalise this sentence.
    may and sam said that they didnt do it miss jones

    _____

Number and Algebra

1.

+	4	0	2	6	8	65
7						

2.

−	8	4	10	2	6	19
1						

3.

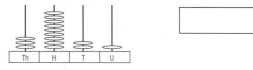

÷	30	45	20	40	10	60
5						

4. What number is represented here?

Th H T U

5. Count on from 3105 in thousands.

[   ] , [   ] , [   ] , [   ]

6. Ted likes pizza. Which fraction would he choose?
$\frac{4}{100}$ or $\frac{40}{100}$

7. 1.25 L soft drinks are on special: 4 bottles for $5. What is the cost of 1 bottle?

8. On Monday I sold 24% of my stock and 39% on Tuesday. How much is left to sell on Wednesday?

9. Iso rounded off 61 572 to 62 000 (nearest thousand). Is the answer True or false?

10. I used 0.38 of my money, then another $\frac{29}{100}$.

What percentage have I left?

Measurement and Geometry

11. My bus took 23 minutes to get to town from my stop. I arrived in town at 9:05 am. When did the bus leave my stop?

12. From 1 kg of onions Mum used 650 g. What mass now remains?

13. Measure the length of this line in millimetres.

14.

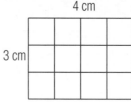

4 cm

3 cm

Martin said this shape has an area of 12 cm². Steve said 7 cm. Who is correct?

15. Write twenty-four cubic centimetres in shortened form.

16. Where in your house could the temperature exceed 100 °C?

17. Draw three concentric circles.

18. Draw a straight angle.

19. For a human face the line of symmetry is vertical / horizontal.

20.

7
6
5
4
3
2 X
1
A B C D E F

↑ N

Start at X. 2 squares North. 3 squares East. 1 square South. The coordinates of this point are:

Statistics and Probability

21. This symbol ✳ represents 20 magazines sold. Interpret Fred's sales on these days.

Monday	✳ ✳ ✕	= [ ]
Tuesday	✳ ✳ ✳ ╲	= [ ]
Wednesday	✳ ✳ ✳	= [ ]
Thursday	✳ ✕	= [ ]
Friday	✳ ✳ ✳ —	= [ ]

22. If 3 coins are tossed at the same time, how many different outcomes are possible?

Computer Holocaust

The year is 2036. Global warfare is raging. Not one country against another. Not even one religious group trying to destroy another. This is all-out war—humans against computers.

Back in 2033—what seems ages ago—the Athan Computer Group (or ACI) perfected a revolutionary new chip that enabled computers to learn. And learn they did—at a rate incomprehensible to humans. Not only did they learn what ACI was about, they linked into the worldwide web of the Internet. Their learning ability spread to other computers, which soon outstripped people's ability in all fields. Computers controlled banking, finance, education, medicine, communication, ... and defence. It happened so quickly no one realised till 29 February 2036 when all computers shut down for the day. I mean all. Chaos reigned supreme. Transport shut down, banks, the Stock Market, businesses ... the lot. The world stood still.

Programmers and technicians tried unsuccessfully to rectify the problem. In frustration one technician picked up a monitor and smashed it into a thousand pieces. One learned behaviour from humans was revenge and that is how it started. Machines began attacking and humans hit back. Now it is all-out war. Luckily the nuclear warheads were removed from all ICBMs under the treaty signed by all countries in 2017, otherwise we'd all be dead. But those warheads are in storage! Who monitors and controls the storage? Noooo ...

Reading and Comprehension

1. The destruction of which computer part started the war? _____

2. In the author's opinion which behaviour, learned from humans, caused this war?

   _____

3. The warfare is between
   (a) one country and another.
   (b) two religious groups.
   (c) ACI and computers.
   (d) humans and computers.

4. How did ACI computers teach other computers?
   (a) through the Internet
   (b) by providing new chips
   (c) through reprogramming
   (d) by using technicians

5. Number these events in chronological order (1–4).
   (a) War was raging.
   (b) A new chip was developed.
   (c) Learning spread through the Internet.
   (d) Computers were taught how to learn.

Spelling and Vocabulary

Rewrite the misspelt words.

6. I though you'd be here on time. _____

7. After the acident he spent weeks in hospital.

   _____

Circle the word that has the nearest meaning to the underlined word.

8. I saw it glistening on the ground.
   (a) shining   (b) lying
   (c) moving   (d) hiding

9. Juan's room is a real jumble.
   (a) picture   (b) muddle
   (c) pleasure   (d) sight

Circle the correct word in brackets.

10. I can't stand to hear you (wrap, rap) your knuckles on the desk.

11. Tasmania is the Apple (Aisle, Isle).

12. The Grecian (earn, urn) was dropped and it broke.

Grammar and Punctuation

13. Use market in a sentence so that it is a **verb**.

    _____

    _____

14. Punctuate and capitalise this sentence.

    whos the thief he demanded

    _____

Number and Algebra

1.

+	1	7	9	4	8	72
9						

2.

−	6	12	8	4	10	81
3						

3.

×	1	7	3	9	5	11
6						

4. What is the value of the 6 in 5067?

5. Continue this pattern:

1, 2 , 4, 8, [   ] , [   ] , [   ]

6. Write the unshaded fraction.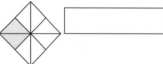

7. A 750 g jar of coffee costs \$8.95; a 375 g jar costs \$4.52. How much will I save by buying the large jar rather than 2 small ones?

8. On a 100 grid, 64 squares are coloured. What percentage of the grid is not coloured?

9. 15 290 rounds off to 15 000 if taken to the nearest hundred. True or false?

10. We left home at 23 minutes past 7. The trip took us 44 minutes. At what time did we arrive?

Measurement and Geometry

11. There are [   ] years in a decade.

12. Correct this statement if necessary.

SPECIAL
Potatoes
5 g for \$1.99

13. 56 millilitres = 56 cm   True or false?

14. What is the best unit to measure the area of a bedroom floor?

15. Write 13 cm^2 in full form.

16. In a freezer you'd expect the temperature to be (more / less) than zero degrees Celsius.

17. A line / line segment / ray has a beginning but no end. Choose the correct term.

18. Measure the size of this angle.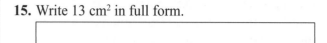

19. A circle has (1 / 2 / 5 / 10 / too many to count) lines of symmetry.

20. 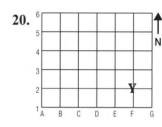 My end point is Y. I went 4 squares South, 2 squares East, 1 square North and 3 squares East. My starting point was:

Statistics and Probability

21. For every 10 people through the gate Jane drew ☺. How many people passed during these hours?

9–10   ☺☺☺☺☺   = [   ]

10–11   ☺☺☺   = [   ]

11–12   ☺☾   = [   ]

12–1   ☾   = [   ]

1–2   ☺☺☺☺☺☺☺   = [   ]

22. List all the possible totals using the two spinners.

Fallen Star

It was a quiet Saturday evening as Jake and his only child Sarah sat on the verandah watching the starry sky.

"Look at that falling star!" exclaimed Sarah the preschooler.

Jake wasn't so sure. He'd seen falling stars before but this was different. It seemed to be getting brighter and slowing down as it 'fell' through the heavens. Suddenly it turned. Jake knew this was no ordinary star. He walked inside; picked up his trusty old 12 gauge; told Sarah to stay inside; loaded the shotgun and headed out.

He could see a glow in the bottom paddock. He trudged over the muddy ground towards the light. As he reached the top of the hill he saw … a blinding flash. He felt weak, fell to his knees and collapsed on the ground.

As Jake awoke he realised it was daylight. He was wet through—rain again. He looked round. There was no glowing light but his head ached. He stood up, then bent down and picked up his shotgun. It was rusty. He needed to give it a good clean, he thought as he headed home. As he approached the homestead he had the feeling that things were different. A teenager ran towards him from the house. As she approached he stared at her. It was Sarah! What had happened?

Reading and Comprehension

1. In which paddock had the fallen star landed?

   _____

2. What is a *12 gauge*? _____

3. Which behaviour of the falling star convinced Jake it wasn't an ordinary falling star?
   (a) It was getting brighter.
   (b) It landed in his paddock.
   (c) It was slowing down.
   (d) It turned.

4. What was the first indication he had that things were different?
   (a) It had rained.
   (b) He had a headache.
   (c) The light had gone.
   (d) His gun was rusty.

5. Number these sentences in order (1–4).
   (a) Jake noticed that his gun was rusty.
   (b) He loaded his shotgun.
   (c) He felt things were different.
   (d) Sarah, his teenager, came up to him.

Spelling and Vocabulary

Rewrite the misspelt words.

6. Have you read 'Tom's Great Addventure'?

   _____

7. Of coarse you can go. _____

Circle the word that has the nearest meaning to the underlined word.

8. He <u>tilted</u> on his chair.
   (a) sat   (b) stood
   (c) leaned   (d) tipped

9. That is an <u>outrageous</u> lie.
   (a) outright   (b) obvious
   (c) unfortunate   (d) shocking

Circle the correct word in brackets.

10. The nail (tore, taw) the shirt.

11. I (did, done) my homework.

12. He has (wrote, written) his name on the wall.

Grammar and Punctuation

13. Write the **plurals** of these **nouns**.

   loaf _____ wife _____

   scarf _____ knife _____

   leaf _____ wharf _____

14. Punctuate and capitalise this sentence.

   in sydney replied bill is the best zoo in australia

   _____

41

Number and Algebra

1. Add 5 to each of these numbers round the circle.

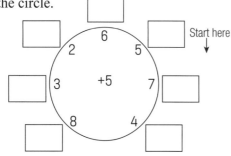

Start here

2. Take 3 from each of these numbers round the circle.

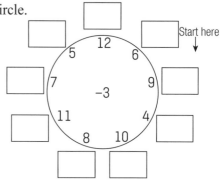

Start here

3. Start with 3, double it, multiply that amount by 4, divide it by 3 and your answer is:

4. Which of these numerals does not represent 5047?
   (a) 5000 + 400 + 7   (b) 4000 + 1040 + 7
   (c) five thousand and forty-seven   (d) 5047 ones

5. Between 680 and 690 there are [   ] odd numbers.

6. I like cake. I was offered 4 tenths or $\frac{40}{100}$ of the cake. Which fraction do you think I chose?

7. Which of these packs of soap powder is the better value?

8. Cross out the one that doesn't belong in the set:

   84%, $\frac{84}{100}$, 8.4, 84 hundredths, eighty-four percent, eighty-four hundredths

9. I have $7\frac{1}{2}$ thousand dollars to spend on a car. The one I want is $7399.
   Round this cost off to the nearest hundred dollars.

10. One can of beans costs $0.78.
    If I buy the whole carton, it will cost:

Measurement and Geometry

11. This is the time we started: **6 : 54** . Our journey took 15 minutes.

    What is the time? Draw it on the clock.

12. Mum bought 2 kg of self-raising flour to make cakes and biscuits. She used $\frac{1}{2}$ kg for the cake, 200 g for one lot of biscuits and $\frac{3}{4}$ kg for the other batches of biscuits. What mass of flour remains?

13. Draw a line here that is exactly 64 mm long.

Answers

UNIT page 8

Maths

1. 14, 13, 11, 8, 7, 41
2. 6, 3, 9, 4, 7, 19
3. 42, 48, 36, 54, 30, 72
4. 5
5. 574, 576
6. $\frac{6}{8}$
7. $2.70
8. 5
9. 700
10. 77
11. 25 minutes to 10
12. 100 g
13. 269 cm
14. 10 cm^2
15. 650 mL
16. 0 °C
17. square
18. A
19. 4
20. (a) F   (b) A   (c) D
21. 30
22. No

English

1. 3
2. In the beginning—Dreaming
3. c
4. a
5. 1b, 2d, 3c, 4a
6. appear
7. believe
8. put
9. almost
10. seen
11. lose
12. sewing
13. apples, bananas, oranges, lemons, trucks, market
14. This is Mr JP Smith.

UNIT page 10

Maths

1. 13, 10, 15, 14, 8, 31
2. 0, 8, 1, 9, 6, 30
3. 6, 4, 2, 10, 8, 16
4. 5087
5. 1023, 1025
6.
7. $3.15
8. 0.29
9. 5000
10. $24.50
11.
12. b
13. 4 m 28 cm
14. 14 cm^2
15. 668 mL
16. thermometer
17. square with a cross in it
18. 4
19. False
20. East
21. a and e
22. very likely

English

1. rain
2. TV
3. d
4. d
5. 1b, 2c, 3d, 4a
6. breakfast
7. centimetre
8. a
9. c
10. there
11. soul
12. would
13. go, jumps, soil
14. The town of Broken Hill is in New South Wales.

UNIT 3 page 12

Maths

1. 15, 14, 10, 12, 17, 21
2. 9, 7, 8, 1, 5, 48
3. 3, 21, 0, 24, 15, 33
4. 6911, 619l, 1691
5. 598, 599
6. $\frac{5}{9}$
7. 200
8. 0.08
9. 400 + 1600 = 2000
10. 126
11. 5 past 11
12. 5
13. 200
14. 17
15. L
16. b
17. 4, 4, 2, 4
18. 2
19. 5
20. a car
21.
22. 1 in 3

English

1. b
2. d
3. telegram
4. gold
5. 1c, 2d, 3b, 4a
6. decide
7. lose
8. c
9. b
10. tears
11. tale
12. hoard
13. I, my
14. Tell Fred I want to see him each Friday in March.

Answers

UNIT 4 page 14

Maths

1. 8, 12, 10, 14, l6, 81
2. 7, 2, 9, 4, 8, 69
3. 6, 9, 5, 7, 8, 12
4. 5623
5. 3600, 3595
6. $\frac{5}{8}$
7. less
8. 0.7
9. 800
10. 73 cents
11.
12. 750 g
13. 16 cm
14. 6.5 cm^2
15. 600 mL
16. rise
17. 0, 4, 1
18. 5, equal
19.   20.
21. 13
22. 0

English

1. Egyptians
2. gold
3. a
4. a
5. 1d, 2c, 3b, 4a
6. favourite
7. machine
8. d
9. d
10. dew
11. where
12. there
13. he, his, I, him
14. Mum bought apples, pears, bananas and oranges from Mr Ling.

UNIT 5 page 16

Maths

1. 10, 17, 12, 16, 13, 44
2. 3, 9, 4, 1, 7, 15
3. 30, 10, 40, 20, 25, 50
4. 400
5. 3588, 3598, 3608
6. $\frac{37}{100}$ *or* 0.37
7. 4: 1×$2, 1×50c, 1×10c, l×5c
8. 0.66
9. 2
10. $16.05
11. 7:20
12. 985 g
13. 6 km
14. 8 cm^2
15. 250 mL
16. 100 ºC
17. 20, 8
18. B
19. hexagon
20. (3, C)
21. (a) $24   (b) $8   (c) $32
22. 1 in 6

English

1. slow and limited movements
2. cloth
3. c
4. d
5. 1b, 2a, 3d, 4c
6. through
7. probably
8. b
9. c
10. seen
11. run
12. break
13. Answers will vary
14. Is your teacher Mr CK Perry?

UNIT 6 page 18

Maths

1. 9, 7, 6, 10, 4, 90
2. 9, 4, 2, 6, 5, 20
3. 6, 8, 4, 9, 7, 12
4. two thousand eight hundred and sixty-four
5. 1736, 1636, 1536
6.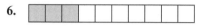
7. $10.55
8. 0.3
9. 6000
10. l6 minutes
11.
12. seven hundred and twenty-eight kilograms
13. 24 m
14. (a) 9 cm^2 (b) 9 cm^2
15. 8200 mL
16. 12 °C
17. heptagon
18.    19.
20. triangle
21. 13 kg
22. 4 outcomes: HH, HT, TH, TT

English

1. geologist
2. Magma below surface, lava above surface.
3. d
4. a
5. 1c, 2d, 3a, 4b
6. plane
7. off
8. d
9. c
10. died
11. pale
12. suite
13. ducks, loaves, roofs, children, oxen
14. Can't you come on Saturday?

Answers

UNIT 7 page 20

Maths

1. 11, 8, 9, 10, 5, 77
2. 7, 2, 9, 6, 3, 26
3. 35, 14, 49, 21, 63, 77
4. 5087
5. 4543, 5543
6.
7. $1.45
8. 0.7
9. 6000
10. 4200 g or 4.2 kg
11. 5:50 or ten to six
12. 48 kg
13. 118 cm
14. 8 cm²
15. 100 mL
16. 34 °C
17. square
18.   19.
20. (D, 6)
21. A and C, B and D
22. Label all the others yellow.

English

1. blue whale
2. swarm
3. c
4. b
5. 1b, 2d, 3a, 4c
6. brought
7. sore
8. a
9. a
10. heard
11. weak
12. place
13. I will be going to my school with him/her.
14. He dived into the cool, clear water.

TEST 1 page 22

Maths

1. 11, 13, 20, 24, 30
2. Final numbers: 1, 4, 11, 2, 4
3. (a) 18, 18, 18, 18 (b) 35, 5, 7
   (c) 0, 0, 0   (d) 64, 8, 64
4. 7342
5. 580, 585, 590
6. $\frac{5}{12}$
7. $6.45
8. check number (52) shaded
9. b
10. 6.325 kg
11.   7:40
12. 480 g
13. (a) 20 cm, 60 cm, 10 cm, 40 cm, 10 cm, 100 cm
    (b) 240 cm
14. 9 squares   15. 100 mL
16. 19 °C   17. a
18. right, acute, obtuse, reflex
19. C and D   20. (4, S)
21. Jenny 7, Joe 32, Mimi 18
22. 36 different outcomes:
    1,1 1,2 1,3 1,4 1,5 1,6 2,1 2,2
    2,3 2,4 2,5 2,6 3,1 3,2 3,3 3,4
    3,5 3,6 4,1 4,2 4,3 4,4 4,5 4,6
    5,1 5,2 5,3 5,4 5,5 5,6 6,1 6,2
    6,3 6,4 6,5 6,6

English

1. notebook, smartphone, laptop
2. hourly
3. c   4. d
5. 1b, 2c, 3a, 4d
6. separated
7. through, through, before
8. a   9. c
10. hear   11. so
12. Its
13. news, radios, listeners, flames, roofs, programs, journalists
14. I heard him say, "At the moment I'm watching my house burn down."

UNIT 8 page 26

Maths

1. 5, 6, 8, 7, 1, 39
2. 6, 8, 5, 2, 7, 44
3. 7, 3, 1, 9, 6, 12
4. 5467
5. 2, 4, 6, 8, 10
6. $\frac{46}{100}$
7. $5.50
8. 74%
9. 4000
10. $1110
11. ten past three in the morning
12. 1056 g, 2875 g
13. 4.28 m
14. 12.5
15. 12
16. 19 °C
17. circle
18. check angle
19. 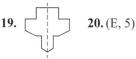   20. (E, 5)
21. Paul $1\frac{1}{2}$ fish, Mary 2 fish, Thomas $2\frac{1}{2}$ fish.
22. 25 heads, 25 tails

English

1. no
2. rot away naturally
3. b
4. all: they all use batteries
5. 1d, 2c, 3a, 4b
6. almost
7. knife
8. a
9. d
10. sung
11. practice
12. brooch
13. teeth, women, mice, geese, feet
14. Did you learn about Asia, Africa, Europe and Australia last year?

Maths

1. 9, 10, 7, 12, 13, 36
2. 9, 12, 14, 1, 8, 53
3. 18, 72, 27, 63, 36, 99
4. 3000 + 800 + 50 + 2
5. 19, 21, 23, 25

6.

7. 8
8. $\frac{65}{100}$ or 65%
9. False
10. $71.65
11. 4:40 pm
12. 640 g
13. 6.4 m
14. (a) m²   (b) cm²
    (c) cm²   (d) m²
15. 27
16. 45 °C
17. 1

18.

19. A‐‐B‐‐C‐‐D
20. (2, C) , (1, B)
21. 110
22. red

English

1. Bactrian
2. True
3. d
4. d
5. 1b, 2d, 3a, 4c
6. month
7. often
8. b
9. a
10. heir
11. coarse
12. current
13. I, my
14. "It is a turtle," replied Jim.

Maths

1. 9, 8, 3, 2, 10, 87
2. 2, 9, 0, 4, 7, 28
3. 6, 1, 7, 9, 4, 8
4. 7609
5. 690, 700, 710, 720
6. $\frac{3}{6}$ or $\frac{1}{2}$
7. 5
8. 0.37, 37%
9. 5874, 6079
10. $7.44
11. 2:35 am
12. less
13. 17.16 m
14. 8 square units
15. 16
16. 36 °C
17. cylinder
18. less
19. false
20. straight line
21. $$$$, $$$$$, $$$$$$$$$$, $$
22. 3

English

1. carbon fibre, sailsheet
2. dowel
3. a or b
4. c
5. 1d, 2a, 3c, 4b
6. happiness
7. friend
8. b
9. a
10. dyeing
11. forth
12. fought
13. The damage to the kite was severe. (Or similar)
14. "It isn't too late," he replied.

Maths

1. 14, 12, 5, 9, 8, 51
2. 2, 8, 0, 4, 6, 25
3. 8, 7, 1, 9, 6, 17
4. 4000 + 400 + 7
5. 3920, 3820, 3720
6. all
7. no
8. 46%
9. 3000
10. 79 L

11.

12. 50 g
13. metres, 8
14. 145 cm²
15. 20
16. 44 °C

17.

18. greater, straight

19.

20. acute
21. 4   22. yellow

English

1. bottom of the ocean
2. 80 billion tonnes
3. d
4. c
5. 1b, 2d, 3a, 4c
6. Wednesday
7. forty
8. a
9. d
10. pain
11. groan
12. whole
13. Don't damage the environment. (Or similar)
14. "Is this a turtle?" asked Sean.

Answers

UNIT ⑫ page 34

Maths

1. 11, 12, 10, 13, 7, 94
2. 1, 9, 0, 6, 8, 27
3. 7, 5, 1, 3, 9, 12
4. 5374
5. 3087
6. $\frac{63}{100}$
7. $9.41
8. 47%, $\frac{47}{100}$
9. 62 000
10. $17.10
11. 12:11 pm
12. 8
13. 21.41 m
14. 1 m²
15.
16. 17 °C
17. sphere
18. reflex
19.
20. (5, C)
21. M – 2½ cars, T – 2, W – 3, T – 1½, F – 3½
22. 30 blue, 30 red, 40 green

English

1. chemicals and gases
2. methane
3. d
4. c
5. 1d, 2b, 3c, 4a
6. trouble
7. woollen
8. a
9. d
10. It's
11. idle
12. We've
13. verb
14. "He did it on purpose," I replied.

UNIT ⑬ page 36

Maths

1. 10, 15, 12, 16, 14, 37
2. 8, 6, 5, 9, 7, 34
3. 56, 8, 72, 24, 40, 96
4.
5. 3597
6. $\frac{13}{100}$, $\frac{30}{100}$, $\frac{33}{100}$
7. $17.50
8. 80%
9. 40 000
10. 258
11. 12:05 am
12. 1625 g or 1.625 kg
13. 4.91 m
14. 3 cm
15. 1 cm³
16. 0 °C, 100 °C
17. a-cone, b-cylinder, c-sphere
18. Acute – A, Right – D, Obtuse – C, Straight – E, Reflex – B
19.
20. north-east
21. 40, 40, 60, 20
22. yes, but not probable

English

1. 3000 years
2. Greece
3. b
4. b
5. 1b, 2d, 3c, 4a
6. piece
7. poem
8. c
9. c
10. steal
11. worn
12. Where's
13. verb
14. May and Sam said that they didn't do it, Miss Jones.

UNIT ⑭ page 38

Maths

1. 11, 7, 9, 13, 15, 72
2. 7, 3, 9, 1, 5, 18
3. 6, 9, 4, 8, 2, 12
4. 3921
5. 4105, 5105, 6105, 7105
6. $\frac{40}{100}$
7. $1.25
8. 37%
9. true
10. 33%
11. 8:42 am
12. 350 g
13. 32 mm
14. Martin
15. 24 cm³
16. stove
17.  18.
19. vertical
20. (E, 3)
21. 50, 65, 60, 30, 65
22. 8 outcomes: HHH, HHT, HTH, THH, TTH, THT, HTT, TTT

English

1. monitor
2. revenge
3. d
4. a
5. 1b, 2d, 3c, 4a
6. thought
7. accident
8. a
9. b
10. rap
11. Isle
12. urn
13. ACI will market the new chip. (or similar)
14. "Who's the thief?" he demanded.

Answers

Maths

1. 10, 16, 18, 13, 17, 81
2. 3, 9, 5, 1, 7, 78
3. 6, 42, 18, 54, 30, 66
4. 60
5. 16, 32, 64
6. $\frac{3}{4}$
7. 9 cents
8. 36%
9. false
10. 8.07
11. 10
12. 5 kg
13. false (56 mL = 56 cm^3)
14. m^2
15. thirteen square centimetres
16. less
17. ray
18. 60°
19. too many to count
20. (A, 5)
21. 50, 30, 15, 5, 70
22. 2, 3, 4, 5, 6, 7, 8

English

1. bottom
2. shotgun
3. d
4. d
5. 1b, 2a, 3c, 4d
6. adventure
7. course
8. c
9. d
10. tore
11. did
12. written
13. loaves, wives, scarves, knives, leaves, wharves
14. "In Sydney," replied Bill, "is the best zoo in Australia."

Maths

1. 10, 12, 9, 13, 8, 7, 11
2. 3, 6, 1, 7, 5, 8, 4, 2, 9
3. 8   4. a
5. 5
6. both the same
7. 2 kg   **8.** 8.4
9. $7400   **10.** $9.36
11.   **12.** 550 g

13. check length 64 mm
14. all
15. 24
16. 0 °C
17. cross-section off a corner
18. a-right, b-obtuse, c-acute, d-acute
19. **S Y M M E T R Y**
20.

21. 60, 40, 30, 50, 80, 60, 10
22. 3 red, 5 green, 2 blue —5 out of 10

English

1. 40   **2.** 1986
3. d   **4.** c
5. 1e, 2a, 3g, 4c, 5b, 6h, 7f, 8d
6. centre, different, sun
7. travelling, plane, marbles, rolling, different
8. d   **9.** c
10. quite
11. further
12. tail
13. The moon will orbit the planet. (or similar)
14. Mercury, Venus, Earth and Mars are rocky planets whereas Jupiter, Saturn, Uranus and Neptune are gaseous.

Maths

1. 8, 7, 10, 6, 2, 33
2. 0, 6, 2, 8, 4, 9
3. 9, 8, 7, 6, 5, 12
4. 57 223
5. 18, 21, 24
6. $\frac{9}{100}$
7. 50 cents
8. 16%
9. 5500
10. 1 km
11. night
12. 178 g
13. 4.06 m
14. 35 m^2
15. 15 cm^3
16. 44 °C
17. ruler
18. 45°
19. no lines of symmetry
20. (C, 1), (A, 3), (D, 6), (F, 4)
21. 800 mL
22. 16 outcomes: HHHH, HHHT, HHTH, HHTT, HTHH, HTHT, HTTH, HTTT, THHH, THHT, THTH, THTT, TTHH, TTHT, TTTH, TTTT

English

1. nose
2. bats will leave
3. a
4. d
5. 1c, 2d, 3a, 4b
6. finally
7. jumped
8. a
9. d
10. rung
11. wring
12. teach
13. He gave a shout of joy.
14. Guy's grandfather owns a winery in the Hunter Valley.

Answers

Maths

1. 6, 7, 4, 10, 5, 79
2. 2, 5, 1, 3, 0, 44
3. 36, 8, 20, 16, 0, 40
4.
5. 18, 26, 36 or 20, 36, 68
6. greater
7. no
8. 72%
9. 250
10. CCCLXXVI
11. 3:42 pm
12. 1×100 g, 3×20 g, 1×10 g, 5×1 g
13. 169
14. 8 cm²
15. 850 cm³
16. 15 °C
17. circle
18. vertical surface
19. true
20. (B, 4)
21. 8°
22. 16: AA, AB, AC, AD, BA, BB, BC, BD, CA, CB, CC, CD, DA, DB, DC, DD

English

1. south
2. study of stars/planets
3. d
4. c
5. 1b, 2c, 3d, 4a
6. straight
7. video
8. b
9. c
10. too
11. beach
12. mail
13. country child
14. When the storm struck did it do much damage?

Maths

1. 9, 8, 6, 4, 0, 35
2. 2, 6, 0, 8, 4, 39
3. 9, 7, 1, 3, 5, 24
4. 26 527
5. 40, 80, 160
6. $\frac{83}{100}$ $\frac{82}{100}$ $\frac{80}{100}$
7. $12.90
8. $\frac{63}{100}$, 63%
9. 630
10. 130
11. 0700, 1200, 1700, 0000
12. a
13. 255
14. 16 m²
15. 6 cm³
16.
17. cylinder
18. protractor
19.
20. triangle
21. Sue, Bill, Ki
22. 4; long sleeved + shorts, long sleeved + trousers, short sleeved + shorts, short sleeved + trousers

English

1. daggy
2. cold and windy
3. chewing ice cubes
4. d
5. 1a, 2b, 3c, 4d
6. animals
7. weather
8. a
9. d   10. straight
11. barren   12. sail
13. in the box, on the counter, from Switzerland
14. Mr CL Jones
    24 Summer St
    Coffs Harbour NSW 2450

Maths

1. 5, 1, 6, 0, 3, 99
2. 4, 0, 6, 2, 9, 59
3. 8, 4, 12, 16, 18, 24
4. 10 000 + 6000 + 80 + 9
5. 76, 68, 60
6. $\frac{5}{10}$
7. $13.50
8. 0.56
9. 20   10. $10.10
11. 0800   12. all same
13. 4.7 cm   14. 8 square units
15. 25   16. 33 °C
17.
18. 0°, 90°
19.
20. (A, 5)   21. Yi
22. 6: ABC, ACB, BAC, BCA, CAB, CBA

English

1. False
2. c
3. a
4. b
5. terracotta, warriors, Mount
6. metres, more, thousand, figures
7. c
8. a
9. shield
10. pyramid
11. wrote
12. The warriors of terracotta were found in pits near Mount Li in China in 1974.
13. Swords, shields, spears, axes and other weapons were found in the pits.

Answers

UNIT 20 page 54

Maths

1. 9, 12, 10, 13, 11, 32
2. 9, 5, 8, 7, 6, 98
3. 7, 6, 5, 8, 3, 14
4. 900
5. 16, 25, 36
6.
7. 4 L
8. $\frac{7}{100}$
9. 60 000
10.

9	2	7
4	6	8
5	10	3

11. 1300   12. 1000 g/ 1 kg
13. millimetres 14. 154 cm²
15. a
16. sixty-four degrees Celsius
17. triangular prism
18. 90
19. 2
20. parallelogram
21.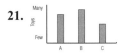

22. SAN, SNA, NSA, ASN, NAS, ANS

English

1. guards
2. John Wilkes Booth
3. b
4. a
5. 1c, 2a, 3d, 4b
6. fourteen
7. Saturdays
8. d
9. a
10. plain
11. been
12. poor
13. John found a shell.
14. Miss Mary Smith
    21 Avondale Ct
    Jondale NSW 2468

UNIT 21 page 56

Maths

1. 9, 6, 11, 8, 3, 37
2. 3, 2, 0, 9, 7, 38
3. 0, 0, 0, 0, 0, 0
4. 95 067
5. 8, 6, 5
6. $\frac{6}{100}$
7. $2.35
8. 61%
9. 18 956
10. 4 × 4 L cans
11.

12. 839 g   13. 2.1 m
14. 36 m²
15. 1000 cm³, 1000 mL
16. 17 °C   17. cone
18. 130°   19. no
20. X(0, B), Y(2, B), Z(0, D)
21. underweight
22. ABC, ACB, BAC, BCA, CAB, CBA

English

1. true
2. Hindu holy men as well as the Khmer people
3. very old
4. (a) inside   (b) is
   (c) elephants (d) surfaces
5. (a) Khmer   (b) 40
   (c) flag   (d) South-East
6. Sandstone, build, temple
7. been, decorated, extensive, carvings
8. a
9. c
10 to
11. It's
12. build
13. Buddhist
14. The stones to build the roofs of the temples were carried by rafts then hauled by elephants.

UNIT 22 page 58

Maths

1. 13, 10, 12, 11, 14, 61
2. 2, 6, 0, 4, 8, 37
3. 5, 1, 7, 3, 9, 11
4. 49 016
5. 11, 13, 14
6. $\frac{80}{100}$
7. no
8. 5%
9. $6
10. $30.20
11. 10 pm
12. a
13. 2.45 m or 245 cm
14. 2 m
15. 127 mL
16. 18 °C
17. vertical
18. obtuse
19. circle
20. (D, 3)
21. false
22. 10

English

1. the purse
2. canine
3. b
4. a
5. b
6. ninety
7. which
8. a
9. d
10. one
11. Bears
12. right
13. Answers will vary, e.g. The mouse <u>with a long tail</u> quickly scampered <u>across the floor</u>.
14. When I'm in Year Eight I'll be as big and strong as Joshua Hall.

Answers

UNIT 23 page 60

Maths

1. 13, 10, 7, 11, 6, 32
2. 7, 3, 9, 1, 5, 66
3. 4, 12, 0, 8, 16, 24
4. ninety-four thousand and forty-nine
5. 31, 36, 41
6. $\frac{79}{100}$
7. $1 \times \$20$, $1 \times \$10$, $1 \times \$5$ or other combinations
8. 75%
9. 13 000
10. 40
11. 2100 hours
12. (a) g   (b) kg   (c) g
13. 8.09 m
14. false
15. 40 cm³
16. 26 ℃
17. square
18. reflex
19. 0, 1, 3, 8
20. (0, F), (1, E), (2, D), (3, C), (4, B)
21. from the 1970s onwards
22. b

English

1. he cheated
2. same
3. a
4. d
5. 1b, 2d, 3a, 4c
6. remember
7. dollar
8. a
9. b
10. eat
11. came
12. guest
13. he, his, he
14. "This," said the hunter, "is the den of the lion."

TEST 3 page 62

Maths

1. 10, 14, 18, 22, 26, 30, 34, 38, 42, 46, 50, 54, 58, 62
2. 24, 21, 18, 15, 12, 9, 6, 3
3. 5, 5, 8, 5, 40
4. 87 430
5. 38, 46, 55
6. 4 tenths, 44 hundredths, $4\frac{0}{10}$
7. $8.55 to nearest cent
8. 40 hundredths
9. 20
10. CCCLXV
11. 7:30 pm or 1930 or
12. 3110 g
13. 70 cm
14. d
15. 22
16. 40.7 ℃
17. c
18. 40°   19. circle
20. (2, C), (3, D), (4, E)
21.   22. HTH, TTT, HHH, THT, TTH, HTT, THH

English

1. mid-1800s   2. Persia
3. c   4. b
5. 1a, 2c, 3b, 4d
6. there, injuries
7. wear, lessen
8. b
9. a
10. raise
11. medal
12. lessen
13. (a) In a hockey team there are eleven players.
    (b) There are, in a hockey team, eleven players.
14. The word 'hockey' appears to have come from the French word *hoquet* which means 'shepherd's crook'.

UNIT 24 page 66

Maths

1. 9, 13, 8, 17, 14, 41
2. 3, 4, 0, 8, 5, 62
3. 8, 5, 7, 4, 6, 11
4. $60\,000 + 6000 + 100 + 60 + 1$
5. 48, 60, 72
6. $\frac{4}{10}$, $\frac{60}{100}$, $\frac{66}{100}$
7. $48.95
8. 1.85
9. 0
10. $8.28
11. 0942
12. 404 kg
13. 1000
14. 7 ha
15. 27
16. 55°
17. shadow on wrong side of tree
18. 3
19. 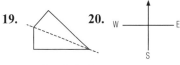   20.
21. on the sixth day
22. 1 in 4

English

1. False
2. very young
3. b
4. b
5. 1a, 2b, 3d, 4c
6. holidays
7. March
8. b
9. d
10. buries
11. pore
12. sheer
13. Paste the two pieces together. (or similar)
14. "Is this," said the hunter, "the den of the lion?"

Answers

UNIT 25 page 68

Maths

1. 14, 11, 16, l2, 13, 60
2. 8, 1, 9, 5, 4, 99
3. 18, 63, 27, 81, 45, 90
4. 94 326
5. 48, 44, 40
6. 0.8 or 0.80
7. $2043
8. 9.13
9. no
10. 1151
11. 8:24 pm
12. 7.265 kg
13. 10 400 m
14. b and c
15. 39 cm³
16.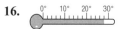
17. 5 m
18. 135º
19. circle
20. north-west
21. 2
22. 2 red, 2 blue, 1 red and 1 blue, 1 blue and 1 red

English

1. 27 April
2. male
3. a
4. c
5. 1b, 2a, 3d, 4c
6. nineteen
7. already
8. d
9. a
10. Aunt
11. sauce
12. weight
13. to, about
14. "Bill," said Gino, "isn't living in Henry Street any more."
    Bill said, "Gino isn't living in Henry Street any more."

UNIT 26 page 70

Maths

1. 13, 16, 18, 15, 14, 47
2. 8, 5, 7, 4, 6, 19
3. 4, 6, 9, 2, 1, 8
4. 800
5. 15, 21, 28
6. 0.7
7. $10.30
8. 25%
9. 3 m
10. 91
11. 1215
12. 3560 g
13. 3 km
14. 5 ha
15. 30 cm³
16. 54 °C
17. b
18. 110º
19. square
20. north-west
21. a-$52, b-$41.60, c-$26, d-$67.60, e-$88.40
22. 50

English

1. Cummie
2. wandering back and forth
3. c
4. d
5. 1d, 2a, 3b, 4c
6. can't
7. caught
8. c
9. b
10. new
11. blue
12. right
13. The bird landed on a branch, sang cheerfully and flew off again.
14. The visitor said, "The gardener is in the hall."
    "The visitor," said the gardener, "is in the hall."

UNIT 27 page 72

Maths

1. 8, 5, 10, 9, 2, 65
2. 9, 5, 2, 0, 4, 59
3. 25, 15, 35, 20, 40, 60
4. A
5. 14, 12, 15
6. $\frac{6}{10}$
7. $1
8. 0.14
9. 7 litres
10. 29.4 L
11. 12:05 pm
12. 6.5 kg
13. 5.647
14. 5 ha
15. 24 mL
16. 37 ºC
17. A
18.   19.
20. north-east
21. (a) 115   (b) 1
22. possible

English

1. to do away with homework
2. revision, discipline, for parents' knowledge or enjoyment
3. c
4. d
5. 1c, 2b, 3d, 4a
6. does
7. Doctor
8. b
9. a
10. Some
11. Where
12. knows
13. At night I will climb into bed, (will) close my eyes and (will) soon go off to sleep.
14. From Coopers Creek Burke, Wills, King and Gray set off for the Gulf of Carpentaria.

Answers

UNIT 28 page 74

Maths

1. 4, 10, 6, 12, 8, 17
2. 4, 8, 2, 6, 9, 37
3. 3, 7, 5, 9, 1, 11
4. 10
5. 498, 500, 502
6. 47 hundredths
7. $8.97
8. 58%
9. 17000
10. $16
11. 0225
12. 7.4 kg
13. Cross out a and c.
14. 36000 m²
15. 135 cm³
16. 8 °C
17. b
18.  19.
20. North-east
21. good
22. unlikely

English

l. flag
2. to find a place to land
3. d
4. a, b, c
5. 1b, 2d, 3c, 4a
6. everything
7. happiness
8. d
9. a
10. tales
11. advice
12. soles
13. brothers-in-law, stepsisters, spoonsful/spoonfuls, men-of-war
14. "What will I do," inquired Tasha, "when the jug is nearly full?"

UNIT 29 page 76

Maths

1. 7, 9, 11, 10, l2, ,33
2. 2, 9, 0, 5, 7, 28
3. 0, 32, 40, 56, 48, 96
4. 39600
5. 4262, 4162, 4062, 3962
6. 1
7. 1 × $5, 1 × $2, 1 × $1 ($1.98 rounded up to $2)
8. 1.38 kg
9. 1000
10. 19 kg
11. 2035
12. 7 kg
13. 4 km
14. 1 m²
15. 1000 cm³
16. 19 °C
17. a circle
18. obtuse
19. no
20. east
21. car 2
22. false

English

1. saying things about a group of people which is not always true
2. minds
3. c
4. b
5. c
6. laser
7. o'clock
8. b
9. c
10. hair
11. fair
12. drunk
13. Flour the meat before cooking. (or similar)
14. My older brother Alfred works as a salesperson for David Jones.

UNIT 30 page 78

Maths

1. 8, 4, 2, 10, 6, 21
2. 2, 1, 4, 0, 3, 49
3. 2, 4, 1, 8, 0, 12
4. 9
5. 1020, 1120, 1220
6. 0.69
7. a
8. 6.83 m
9. 8
10. Paul $7, Lu $8, Pedro $6
11. twenty to three
12. 3140 g or 3.140 kg
13. 4.5 km
14. 1 ha
15. 60 cm³, 60 mL
16. a – 100 °C, b – 37 °C, c – 0 °C
17. higher near Jane than where Jim is
18.
19. True
20. south
21. Wednesday
22. more combinations: 12-(6,6), 7-(6,1) (5,2) (4,3) (3,4) (2,5) (1,6)

English

1. 1988
2. United States
3. b
4. a
5. lc, 2a, 3b, 4d
6. quiet
7. tired
8. a   9. a
10. tide   11. Here's
12. scent
13. The elderly gentleman with a video camera approached the narrow bridge across the creek.
14. Mrs CL Fellows
    Coomoomie
    MS 48
    Glen Innes 2568

Answers

Maths

1. 10, 14, 19, 28
2. 14
3. 42
4. more
5. 55, 80, 110
6. 0.09 $\left(\frac{9}{100}\right)$
7. $29.60
8. 91.1 (only decimal point is changed)
9. $4
10. 75 g
11. 8:40 pm,
12. more than 800 g but less than 1 kg
13. 1000 m or 1 km
14. 75 000 m²
15. same
16. 19.4°
17. same length—optical illusion
18. hexagonal prisms
19. Pine trees tend to be more symmetrical, but not completely so.
20.

East	West	South
←	→	↑

21. a-triathlete, b-horse, c-4WD
22. Untrue. Even: 1,1 1,3 1,5 2,2 2,4 2,6 3,1 3,3 3,5 4,2 4,4 4,6 5,1 5,3 5,5 6,2 6,4 6,6 = 18 results. Odd: 1,2 1,4 1,6 2,1 2,3 2,5 3,2 3,4 3,6 4,1 4,3 4,5 5,2 5,4 5,6 6,1 6,3 6,5 = 18 results

English

1. damper
2. eating bush food
3. b
4. a
5. 1c, 2a, 3b
6. two, were
7. more, vegetables, past
8. a
9. c
10. too
11. suited
12. meat
13. Aboriginal people will survive on bush foods. They will gather berries, (will) hunt animals and (will) catch fish.
14. "Ludwig Leichhardt, an Australian explorer, survived in the desert by eating native birds, animals and fruit," reported Jane.

ANSWERS: *Excel* Basic Skills English and Mathematics Year 5

14. Which of these shapes has an area of 1 m²?

(a)

(b)

(c)

15. How many cubes of 1 cm³ would be able to be packed inside this shape?

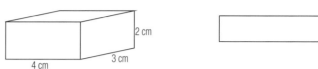

16. Frost forms when dew freezes. This means the grass temperature must be [   ] °C or less.

17. How can I cut a cross-section from this shape to form a triangle?

18. Name the types of angles in this shape.

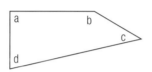

(a)   (b)

(c)   (d)

19. Draw in the lines of symmetry in the letters of this word.   **S Y M M E T R Y**

20.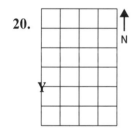

Y is your starting position. Go North 2 squares. Turn East for 3 squares. Now South 4 squares and finally West 1 square. Mark this spot with an 'X'.

Statistics and Probability

21. 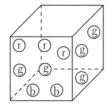 represents 20 bags of flour.

Calculate how many bags of flour our baker uses each day.

S =

M =

T =

W =

T =

F =

S =

22.

In this box there are [   ] red balls, [   ] green balls and [   ] blue balls.

If I draw out a ball, then put it back and continue redrawing, what are my chances of pulling out a green ball? Circle the correct probability.
(5 out of 5 / 3 out of 10 / 5 out of 10 / 5 out of 7)

The planets and other solid matter

Our solar system has just one large sun in its centre, and many different objects that go around this sun. Although it seems to be quite simple, our solar system is in fact a very complicated structure.

The planets all go around the Sun in the same direction. They are all travelling in practically the same plane, like marbles rolling around on a plate, in different-sized circles. All together, the planets have at least 146 moons revolving around them.

Mercury, Venus, Earth and Mars are the four inner planets. They are small, rocky planets close to the Sun, with diameters ranging from 5000 to 13000 kilometres.

The four outer planets are not rocky at all. Jupiter, Saturn, Uranus and Neptune are almost all gas and are about ten times as big as the inner planets. Although Saturn is most well-known for its spectacular rings, each of the outer gas giants also has a set of rings. These rings are about one kilometre thick, and are made from rocks and blocks of ice about the size of a car or fridge. Each of the outer planets has at least six moons orbiting around it—just like a miniature solar system.

There are a few bands of asteroids between the inner and outer planets. These asteroids range from a few metres across to 1000 kilometres—from the size of a car to the size of New South Wales.

After the four outer planets is a belt of frozen bodies, including the dwarf planet Pluto. Pluto takes about 247 Earth years to do a complete loop around the Sun. Astronomers call the

average distance from the Earth to the Sun one Astronomical Unit (AU). Pluto is about 40 AU from the Sun.

Further out, astronomers think there may be two spherical clouds of 'sleeping comets'. They suggest that in these clouds lumps of dirty ice, the size of mountains, wheel slowly around a very distant sun. A few of them fall towards our Sun. As they draw close, they heat up and begin to show a tail. We then see them in the sky, like Halley's Comet, which last appeared in 1986.

Reading and Comprehension

1. Pluto is _____ Astronomical Units from the Sun.

2. In which year did Halley's Comet last appear?

_____

3. Which of these features is not found in our solar system?
(a) planets   (b) Sun
(c) moons   (d) galaxies

4. The planets are similar in that they all
(a) are about the same size.
(b) have moons orbiting them.
(c) travel around the Sun in the same direction.
(d) are made of rock.

5. Number the eight planets in order from closest to furthest from the Sun.
(a) Venus   (b) Jupiter
(c) Mars   (d) Neptune
(e) Mercury   (f) Uranus
(g) Earth   (h) Saturn

Spelling and Vocabulary

Rewrite the misspelt words.

6. Our solar system has just one large sun in its center and many diferent objects that go around this son.

_____

_____

_____

7. They are all traveling practically in the same plain, like marbels roling around on a plate, in diffrent-sized circles.

_____

_____

_____

Circle the word that has the nearest meaning to the underlined word.

8. Our solar system is in fact a very complicated structure.
(a) simple
(b) usual
(c) common
(d) difficult to understand

9. Saturn is best known for its spectacular rings.
(a) easily seen
(b) in the shape of spectacles
(c) striking
(d) made of rocks and ice

Circle the correct word in brackets.

10. The solar system seems to be (quiet, quite) simple.

11. (Further, Father) out from the asteroids are the clouds of sleeping comets.

12. As they draw close, they begin to heat up and show a (tale, tail).

Grammar and Punctuation

13. Use the word *orbit* in a sentence so that it is a **verb**.

_____

_____

_____

14. Rewrite this sentence with correct punctuation and capitalisation.

mercury venus earth and mars are rocky planets whereas jupiter saturn uranus and neptune are gaseous

_____

_____

_____

_____

Mathematics

Number and Algebra

1.

+	7	6	9	5	1	32
1						

2.

−	2	8	4	10	6	11
2						

3.

÷	72	64	56	48	40	96
8						

4. Write the numeral for:

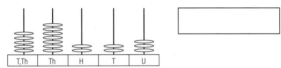

5. Complete the pattern:

9, 12, 15, [   ], [   ], [   ]

6. Select the fraction with the least value.

$\frac{9}{100}$ $\frac{90}{100}$ $\frac{99}{100}$

7. Six cans sell for $2.99. What would one can cost? (Round off your answer.)

8. 84% of a drum of oil has been used. What % remains?

9. Give an approximate answer for:

$$3574 + 1892$$

10. Margie swims 40 laps of the 25 metre pool each day. How far is this in kilometres?

Measurement and Geometry

11. Why would you not expect to see sunlight at 3:45 am?

12. A scale is balanced when a block of wood is placed on one side and these masses—1×100 g 1×50 g, 1×20 g, 1×5 g and 3×1 g—are placed on the other side. What is the mass of the block of wood?

13. Write 4 metres and 6 centimetres in decimal form.

14. Convert the 700 cm to metres and then calculate the area of the rectangle.

15. I had 180 mL of water in a measuring cylinder. I added a stone. The reading is now 195 mL. What is the volume of the stone?

16. Write forty-four degrees Celsius in abbreviated form.

17. Cross out the name(s) of the instrument(s) that do not tell if a surface is vertical.
plumb-bob   level   ruler

18. Measure this angle.

19. Draw in the line(s) of symmetry in this shape.

20. 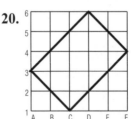 List the coordinates of the 4 corners of this rectangle.

Statistics and Probability

21. 4 cups have a volume of:

22. List the possible outcomes when 4 coins are tossed.

Orange horseshoe bat

The orange (or golden) horseshoe bat lives in tropical (warm and moist) caves in northern Australia. The temperature in the caves ranges from 28°C to 32°C, with 92 to 100 per cent humidity. This bat has been found in eight caves in the Northern Territory, and one in the Kimberley region of Western Australia.

The orange horseshoe bat weighs about 9 grams, and its forearms are about 5 centimetres long. It has bright orange fur, a circular nose shaped like a horseshoe, and small pointed ears. Its breeding habits are unknown.

The bat is silent and nocturnal (active at night). At dusk it leaves the cave to feed, mostly on moths, but it also eats beetles, wasps, ants and weevils. It returns to the cave often to groom (clean its fur), digest its food and sleep.

Scientists think this bat is rare. Probably there are about 34 000 of them altogether. The largest colony—29 000 bats—lives in a cave at Tolmer Falls in Litchfield Park, 100 kilometres south of Darwin.

The cave is surrounded by rainforest. Near the opening, water pours over high cliffs into a deep pool. It is a beautiful place, and many tourists would like to see it. However, the bats are afraid of people. When people enter a cave in which bats are living, the bats move away, deeper into the cave. A colony of bats may leave a cave altogether if humans continue to visit. This happened at Katherine, Northern Territory.

Therefore, the Northern Territory Conservation Commission has decided to destroy the four-wheel drive track that leads to the falls.

Reading and Comprehension

1. What part of the bat gives it its 'horseshoe' name?

   _____

2. What will happen if too many humans visit the home (cave) of orange horseshoe bats?

   _____

3. Why did the Northern Territory Conservation Commission destroy the 4-wheel drive track to Tolmer Falls?
   (a) to protect the bats

   (b) to keep tourists away from danger
   (c) to stop people seeing the falls
   (d) because the road was too dangerous

4. The word *nocturnal* means
   (a) 'very rare'.   (b) 'living in tropical areas'.
   (c) 'makes no noise'.   (d) 'active at night'.

5. Match these statements.
   (1) Forearms are   (a) moths.
   (2) One bat has a mass of   (b) 28 to 32°C.
   (3) Its major food source is   (c) 5 cm long.
   (4) Most favoured temperature   (d) 9 grams.
        range is

Spelling and Vocabulary

Rewrite the misspelt words.

6. Finaly you understand what I want. _____

7. Mike jumpt over the log. _____

Circle the word that has the nearest meaning to the underlined word.

8. We met them at the <u>temple</u>.
   (a) church   (b) hall   (c) theatre   (d) hotel

9. The cows were all <u>branded</u>.
   (a) sold   (b) dipped   (c) bought   (d) marked

Circle the correct word in brackets.

10. The bell was (rang, rung).

11. (Ring, Wring) out the clothes before they go on the line.

12. (Teach, Learn) me the piano.

Grammar and Punctuation

13. Change the underlined words into a **phrase**.

    He gave a <u>joyful shout</u>.

    _____

14. Punctuate and capitalise this sentence correctly.
    guys grandfather owns a winery in the hunter valley

    _____

    _____

Number and Algebra

1.

+	3	4	1	7	2	76
3						

2.

−	11	14	10	12	9	53
9						

3.

×	9	2	5	4	0	10
4						

4. Show 62 854 on this abacus.

5. Complete the pattern:

6, 8, 12, ☐ , ☐ , ☐

6. Is $\frac{64}{100}$ greater/less than $\frac{46}{100}$?

7. I have 3 × 50c coins, 2 × $1 coins, 1 × $2 coin and six five cent coins. Have I enough to pay $5.90 for my lunch?

8. I've saved up 28% of the cost of a new bike. What % have I still to save?

9. Estimate the answer to:
398
− 147

10. Find the answer to this addition of Roman numerals and write it in Roman numerals.
CCXIX + CLVII

Measurement and Geometry

11. Which is the later time in the afternoon?
3:42 pm / 20 to four

12. How many of each of these masses will have to be placed in the right-hand pan to balance the scale?
100 g, 20 g, 10 g, 1 g

13. 1.69 m = ☐ cm

14. Correct this statement if necessary:
The area of this rectangle is 8 metres.

4 cm
2 cm

15. Write eight hundred and fifty cubic centimetres in short form.

16. What is the difference between 17 °C and 32 °C?

17. Every elevation (or view) of a sphere is a:

18. Name the surface that is 90° to a horizontal surface.

19. In a rectangle a vertical bisecting line is a line of symmetry. True or false?

20.

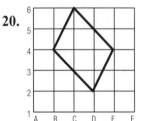

The corners of this shape are (C, 6), (E, 4), (D, 2) and:

Statistics and Probability

21.

What was the temperature at 6 pm?

22. There are 4 flavours of ice cream. You can have a double. How many different ways can the cone be made? (Let A, B, C and D stand for the 4 flavours.)

The life of George Smith

My name is George Smith. I was born in Newcastle, my father being employed as a gardener in the grounds of a large estate just outside the city. My mother died when I was eleven and my father passed away when I was thirteen. My uncle, Edward Brown, came north from Sydney and adopted me as his own son. He was a single man and very well known in the capital city as a successful newspaper journalist and a very keen student of astronomy. For several years I lived happily with my uncle, and at his death, which happened only four years ago, he left me his entire fortune, which amounted to the huge sum of two hundred thousand dollars.

I was twenty-two at that time and greatly interested in the pop music scene. I returned to the city in which I spent my childhood. Here I met up with an old friend from my school days. What started out as a bit of a joke over a drink or two has now, a year later, become a flourishing partnership in, of all things, a florist shop.

Reading and Comprehension

1. Is Sydney north or south of Newcastle?

   _____

2. What is astronomy?

   _____

3. What age was George Smith
   when he wrote this passage?
   (a) eleven   (b) thirteen
   (c) twenty-two   (d) twenty-six

4. Edward Brown was
   (a) George's father.
   (b) George's father's brother.
   (c) George's mother's brother.
   (d) George's father's father.

5. Number these events in George's life (1–4).
   (a) forming a partnership
   (b) becoming an orphan
   (c) being adopted by his uncle
   (d) being interested in the pop music scene

Spelling and Vocabulary

Rewrite the misspelt words.

6. You are to go strait home. _____

7. Come and play on my vidio game. _____

Circle the word that has the nearest meaning to the underlined word.

8. The knot was very <u>firm</u>.
   (a) neat   (b) tight
   (c) loose   (d) old

9. Will you <u>exchange</u> toys with me?
   (a) buy   (b) look at
   (c) trade   (d) sell

Circle the correct word in brackets.

10. (To, Too, Two) many questions are asked by you.

11. We had fun on the (beach, beech) in the sand.

12. (Mail, Male) this letter for me.

Grammar and Punctuation

13. Rewrite this sentence using **one word** instead of the underlined phrase.

    The child <u>from the country</u> found city life very hectic.

    _____

14. Punctuate and capitalise this sentence correctly.

    when the storm struck did it do much damage

    _____

    _____

    _____

Number and Algebra

1.

+	9	8	6	4	0	35
0						

2.

−	9	13	7	15	11	46
7						

3.

÷	18	14	2	6	10	48
2						

4. Write one numeral for:
$20\,000 + 6000 + 500 + 20 + 7$

5. Complete the pattern:

5, 10, 20, _____ , _____ , _____

6. Order these from greatest to least:

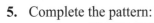
$\frac{80}{100}$ $\frac{83}{100}$ $\frac{82}{100}$

7. Bottles of drink are on sale at 2 for $2.15. What will a dozen cost?

8. $0.63 = \dfrac{}{100} = \boxed{}\%$

9. Give an approximate answer to: 71×9

10. I counted the heads of 28 sheep and 9 kangaroos—a total of 37. If I counted feet, my total would be:

Measurement and Geometry

11. Write these times in 24 hour form.

(a) 7:00 am _____   (b) midday _____

(c) 5 pm _____   (d) midnight _____

12. Which container is the heaviest? _____

(a) a margarine tub filled with sand
(b) a margarine tub filled with sawdust

13. 25.5 cm = _____ mm

14. The area of this square is:

4 m

15. 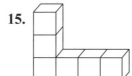 Each cube has a volume of 1 cubic centimetre. Calculate the volume of this shape.

16. Mark 27 °C on this thermometer.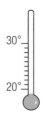

30°

20°

17. 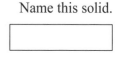 Name this solid.

Top view   Side elevation

End elevation

18. The instrument used to measure angles is a:

19. Draw in the lines of symmetry in this semicircle.

20. 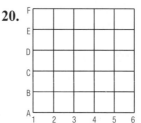 Plot the points (6, B), (3, F) and (2, B). Join the points. Name the shape formed.

Statistics and Probability

21. List the three children in descending order of height.

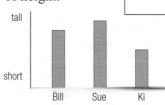

tall

short

Bill   Sue   Ki

22. The school uniform has 2 shirts, long-sleeved and short-sleeved, and 2 pairs of pants, shorts and trousers. How many different ways can Ben wear them?

Thursday 13th April

Dear Diary,

8:50: I'm in make-up, and I have just changed for my first scene. I have a school uniform on. It's blue. My own school doesn't have a uniform. Boy, am I glad! This outfit is the FITS! I've got these really daggy black shoes and grey socks, and the skirt is so short my knees are purple from the cold.

The sun is out today and if I can find a little pozzie away from the wind, then it's sorta warmish. The crew look funny—like they're going to Antarctica.

10:15: Morning tea break. 'Cuppa soup' time. Mushroom. My favourite. Sharon is setting some arithmetic work for me, so while I drink this I'll tell you about my scenes this morning. Not easy. My breath was coming out in clouds and do you know what they did to stop it? I had to chew ice cubes!!! Yoweee it was SO cold on my teeth. Fixed up the problem though. Richard was really happy with me. NOW you know why I'm having hot soup. Oh oh! Sharon's just given me my school work. Back later.

Sharon's gone out of the van for 5 minutes. I can't do this arithmetic. I HATE IT!!! I'll take my time because I know they want me on set at 11:00. Hope they're not running late today. Oops, Sharon's back!

Reading and Comprehension

1. Which word tells you the shoes are not fashionable? _____

2. Describe the climate this morning.

   _____

3. How did they stop the breath coming out in clouds?

   _____

4. Sharon is
   (a) the mother.   (b) the make-up person.
   (c) the wardrobe person. (d) the tutor.

5. Number these sentences in order (1–4).
   (a) Get dressed in a school uniform.
   (b) Get make-up on.
   (c) Film the scenes.
   (d) Have morning tea break.

Spelling and Vocabulary

Rewrite the misspelt words.

6. There were many aminals at the Zoo. _____

7. The wether at this time of year is quite warm.

   _____

Circle the word that has the nearest meaning to the underlined word.

8. She twirled the baton in her hand.
   (a) spun   (b) held
   (c) took   (d) bent

9. The dog strayed from camp.
   (a) hid   (b) barked
   (c) ran   (d) wandered

Circle the correct word in brackets.

10. Come (straight, strait) home.

11. This soil is (barren, baron).

12. I saw a (sale, sail) on the horizon.

Grammar and Punctuation

13. Underline the **phrases** in this sentence.

    In the box on the counter are lollies from Switzerland.

14. Punctuate and capitalise this address.

    mr cl jones
    24 summer st
    coffs harbour nsw 2450

    _____

    _____

    _____

Number and Algebra

1.

+	5	1	6	0	3	99
0						

2.

−	11	7	13	9	16	66
7						

3.

×	4	2	6	8	9	12
2						

4. Expand 16 089.

5. Continue the pattern:

100, 92, 84, _____ , _____ , _____

6. Which is the greatest?

$\frac{4}{10}$ $\frac{44}{100}$ $\frac{5}{10}$

7. Pads cost $1.35.
What will I pay for 10 pads?
$10.35 / $13.50 / $13.05

8. Write 56% as a decimal.

9. When 157 is divided by 8 the answer should be approximately:

10. $60.60 is shared between six.
How much each?

Measurement and Geometry

11. Show 8:00 am on this
24 hour digital face.   :

12. I have 3 bags. The first has 1000 g of gold in it.
The second has 1 kg of feathers and the third
has two 500 g masses.
Which bag is heaviest?

13. 47 mm = _____ cm

14. 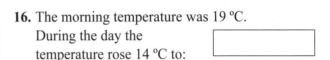 Calculate the area of the shaded triangle.

15. Centicubes have a volume of 1 cm³. How many
centicubes were added to a measuring cylinder
of water if the water level
rose by 25 mL?

16. The morning temperature was 19 °C.
During the day the
temperature rose 14 °C to:

17. Draw the top view of this solid.

18. An acute angle is greater than _____
but less than _____ .

19. Draw a triangle that has
3 lines of symmetry.

20. 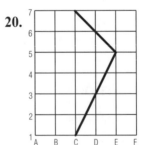 Name the missing point
needed to create a
symmetrical
quadrilateral.

Statistics and Probability

21.  Who has the least
amount to spend?

22. In how many ways can
I arrange 3 children
(A, B and C)?

Terracotta Warriors

In 1974 a group of farmers digging a well near Mount Li in Central China uncovered enough terracotta (unglazed baked clay) fragments to convince archaeologists to investigate. They found a huge collection of pottery figures.

The figures were found in pits near an earthen pyramid built as a tomb for the first Emperor of the Qin dynasty. The historian Sima Qian (145–90 BC) recorded that work on his burial place with palaces, towers, valuable artefacts and wonderful objects began in 246 BC when the Emperor Qin was 13 years old.

The complex was made up of the main burial area (a model of the Imperial Palace), a number of central pits and four other big pits. One of the surrounding pits was 230 metres long and 62 metres wide, containing the main army of more than 6000 figures. The others contained statues of cavalry, infantry, war chariots and officers.

Metal weapons such as swords (still sharp, bright and shiny even after being buried for 2000 years), spears, battle-axes, scimitars, shields, crossbows and arrowheads were found in the pits with the terracotta warriors.

When completed, the life-sized terracotta figures, painted with bright colours with their weapons such as spears, swords or crossbows, were placed in the pits in precise military formation according to rank and duty.

Reading and Comprehension

1. The terracotta warriors were made in 1974. True or false?

2. This tomb was built for
   (a) Sima Qian.
   (b) Mount Li.
   (c) Emperor Qin.
   (d) an ancient empress.

3. In your opinion, why were the terracotta warriors created?
   (a) to guard the Emperor in his afterlife
   (b) to show the people of China how rich and famous he was
   (c) to make work for the many potters in the district
   (d) so that the people of today would know what these people looked like

4. Circle the one statement that is correct.
   (a) The terracotta warriors were made in one piece and arranged in order of height.
   (b) The painted terracotta figures were arranged in order of rank and importance.
   (c) Not only were terracotta statues of men found but also ones made from bronze.
   (d) Over 16 000 terracotta figures were found in the tomb in earthen pyramids.

Spelling and Vocabulary

Rewrite the misspelt words.

5. The teracotta wariors were found near Mountt Li.

_____

6. One pit was 230 meters long and contained mour than six thosand figuers.

_____

Circle the phrase that best fits the meaning of the underlined word.

7. The archaeologist examined the fired piece of clay.
   (a) person who records history
   (b) person who knows about old weapons
   (c) person who studies old civilisations
   (d) person who designs terracotta statues

8. The figures were assembled later.
   (a) put together   (b) arranged in order
   (c) painted with bright colours   (d) fired in a kiln

Circle the correct word in brackets.

9. The warrior used his (shield, sheild) to protect himself.

10. His tomb was built in the shape of a (piramid, pyrmid, pyramid).

11. The historian Sima Qian (wrote, rote, written) about the terracotta warriors.

Grammar and Punctuation

12. Underline the **phrases** in this sentence.

The warriors of terracotta were found in pits near Mount Li in China in 1974.

13. Place **commas** where needed in this sentence.

Swords shields spears axes and other weapons were found in the pits.

Number and Algebra

1.

+	5	8	6	9	7	28
4						

2.

−	9	5	8	7	6	98
0						

3.

÷	7	6	5	8	3	14
1						

4. What is the value of the 9 in 47 956?

5. Continue the pattern:

   1, 4, 9, ____, ____, ____

6. Shade the shape to match the fraction $\frac{8}{9}$.

7. Which gives better value?

8. Circle the fraction that does not belong.

   0.7   70% $\frac{7}{100}$

9. Round off 64 059 to the nearest ten thousand.

10. Use the numbers 2 to 10 once only in each square so that all rows, columns and diagonals add up to 18.

Measurement and Geometry

11. Write the 24 hour time for one hour after midday.

12. One mL of water has a mass of 1 gram, so a litre of water has a mass of:

13. That banana is 210 _____ long.

    Which unit is missing?

14. 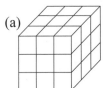 What is the area of this shape in square centimetres?

15. Which of these two shapes made from centicubes has the greater volume?

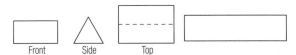

(a)   (b)

16. Write 64 °C in full form.

17. These are three views. What is the name of the shape?

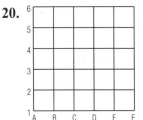

    Front   Side   Top

18. A right angle contains exactly _____ degrees.

19. A rhombus has 0 / 1 / 2 / 3 / 4 lines of symmetry. Circle the correct one.

20. Join these points in order: (B, 2), (E, 1), (E, 5) and (B, 6). Name the shape formed.

Statistics and Probability

21. Draw in the bars to show that A has more choices than C, but fewer than B.

22. I have 3 trophies—for swimming, athletics and netball. List all the different ways I can arrange them on my shelf.

Abraham Lincoln's Tragic Dream

Can people really see into the future? Can dreams foretell disaster as well as good fortune?

This story about President Lincoln was written down in 1865 by one of his close friends, Ward Hill Lamon, just as the President told it.

About 10 days ago I retired very late. I soon began to dream. There seemed to be a deathlike stillness about me. Then I heard subdued sobs, as if a number of people were weeping. I thought I left my bed and wandered downstairs. I went from room to room. No living person was in sight but the same mournful sounds of distress met me as I passed along. I kept on until I arrived at the East Room, where I met with a sickening surprise. I saw a corpse wrapped in funeral vestments. Around it were stationed soldiers who were acting as guards and there was a throng of people weeping pitifully.

"Who is dead in the White House?" I demanded of one of the soldiers. "The President," was his answer. "He was killed by an assassin."

A few days after that account, on 14 April, Lincoln was shot dead by John Wilkes Booth at Ford's Theatre in Washington. His body was taken to lie in the East Room of the White House.

Reading and Comprehension

1. For what purpose were the soldiers at the funeral?

    _____

2. Name the assassin of Abraham Lincoln.

    _____

3. Lincoln had his tragic dream
    (a) ten days before his death.
    (b) about two weeks before his death.
    (c) four days before his death.
    (d) on 14 April.

4. Lincoln was assassinated in
    (a) Ford's Theatre.
    (b) the East Room.
    (c) the White House.
    (d) Ward Hill.

5. Number these statements in order (1–4).
    (a) Ward Hill Lamon recorded the dream.
    (b) Lincoln was assassinated.
    (c) Lincoln recounted his dream.
    (d) Lincoln went to Ford's Theatre.

Spelling and Vocabulary

Rewrite the misspelt words.

6. My brother will be forteen next birthday.

    _____

7. I like Satardays best.

    _____

Circle the word that has the nearest meaning to the underlined word.

8. The soldiers underlined advanced. _____
    (a) stopped   (b) ran away
    (c) rushed forward   (d) moved forward

9. It was a perilous climb. _____
    (a) dangerous   (b) steep
    (c) perpendicular   (d) easy

Circle the correct word in brackets.

10. This (plane, plain) is watered by the Darling River.

11. I haven't (bean, been) well lately.

12. Please give to the (pour, poor).

Grammar and Punctuation

13. Rewrite this sentence, leaving out the **phrases**.

    Among the pebbles on the beach John found a shell with unusual markings on it.

    _____

    _____

14. Punctuate, capitalise and correctly set out this address.

    miss mary smith 21 avondale ct jondale nsw 2468

    _____

    _____

    _____

Number and Algebra

1.

+	7	4	9	6	1	35
2						

2.

−	8	7	5	14	12	43
5						

3.

×	7	6	8	5	3	99
0						

4. $5000 + 90\,000 + 60 + 7$ can be written as:

5. Complete the pattern:

20, 15, 11, _____ , _____ , _____

6. Which has the least value?

$\frac{6}{10}$ $\frac{66}{100}$ $\frac{6}{100}$

7. Toy cars are $2.55. If Thomas buys 3, what change will he get from $10?

8. Convert 0.61 into a percentage.

9. Circle the number closest to 20 000.
18 956   18 569   18 695

10. I need 13 litres of paint. I could buy:

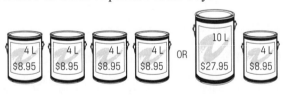

OR

Which is the cheaper way?

Measurement and Geometry

11. **23:00** on an analogue clock is

12. An empty 750 mL glass bottle has a mass of 89 g. When it is full of water it has a mass of:

13. The gateway is 2.1 cm wide.
Correct the statement if necessary.

14. 6 m — Sava calculated the area of the square to be 24 m². Correct the answer if necessary.

15. A centicube has a mass of 1 g and a volume of 1 cm³ and 1 mL. So a large cube weighing 1 kg would have a volume of:
_____ cm³ or a capacity of _____ mL

16. It is 32 °C. The temperature drops 11 °C and then another 4 °C.
The temperature now is:

17. Here are three cross-sections of the same solid. Name it.

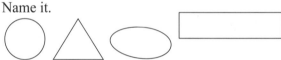

18. 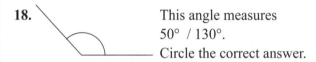 This angle measures 50° / 130°.
Circle the correct answer.

19. Will this pattern tessellate? Yes or no?

20. 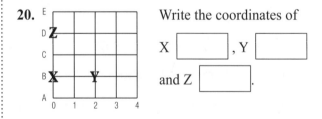 Write the coordinates of
X _____ , Y _____
and Z _____ .

Statistics and Probability

21. This line shows the average mass for height of people.
Is Tom (overweight/ underweight) for his height?

22. 3 people (A, B, C) are in a race. List the possible placings.

Angkor Wat

Angkor Wat (or City Temple) is the largest and best preserved of the ancient structures of Cambodia, South-East Asia. This country's largest religious building was built by the Khmer people for King Suryavarman II (1113–1150) as his state temple and capital city. Ever since then it has remained a significant religious centre—first as Hindu, then as Buddhist.

The huge complex has an outer wall 1024 metres long, 802 metres wide and 4.5 metres high. Inside this is a 30-metre wide strip of open ground surrounding a wide moat.

The sandstone used to build this temple was quarried at Mt Kulen, 40 km away. The blocks of stone are believed to have been put in place by elephants. The whole structure took no more than 40 years.

Extensive carved decorations appear on virtually all the stone surfaces—walls, columns and even roofs.

Today Angkor Wat is a World Heritage site and has become a major tourist destination. It is a symbol of Cambodia and appears on its national flag.

Reading and Comprehension

1. Angkor Wat is rectangular in shape.
   True or false?

2. When Angkor Wat was first built it was used by
   (a) Buddhist monks.
   (b) Hindu Holy Men as well as the Khmer people.
   (c) the Portuguese and the French.
   (d) the Cambodians.

3. The word *ancient* means
   (a) 'very large'.
   (b) 'very old'.
   (c) 'very well built'.
   (d) 'very costly'.

4. Select the word that makes the statement correct.
   (a) The moat is (inside/outside) the outer wall.
   (b) Angkor Wat (is/will be) listed as a World Heritage site.

(c) Most of the stone used to build Angkor Wat was hauled by (elephants/the workers).
(d) All of the stone (walls/surfaces) are carved.

5. Fill in the missing words.
   (a) King Suryavarman II was the leader of the _____ people.
   (b) The complex took _____ years to build.
   (c) A drawing of Angkor Wat is to be seen on the _____ of Cambodia.
   (d) Cambodia is a country in _____-_____ Asia.

Spelling and Vocabulary

Rewrite the misspelt words.

6. Sanstone was used to built the tempel.
7. The stone has bean decoratd with extensif cravings.

Circle the word that has the nearest meaning to the underlined word.

8. We saw the tourists at the temple.
   (a) church
   (b) hall
   (c) hotel
   (d) theme park

9. The castle was surrounded by a moat.
   (a) tall wooden fence
   (b) number of iron gates
   (c) deep ditch filled with water
   (d) many sharp pointed wooden stakes

Circle the correct word in brackets.

10. Have you been (to/too/two) Angkor Wat?
11. (Its/It's) something really worth seeing.
12. Thousands must have worked long and hard to (build/built) this complex.

Grammar and Punctuation

13. Use **one word** instead of this phrase.
    A follower of the teachings of Buddha is called a _____.

14. Change all of the words necessary to make this sentence **plural**.
    The stone to build the roof of the temple was carried by a raft, then hauled by an elephant.

Number and Algebra

1.

+	8	5	7	6	9	56
5						

2.

−	8	12	6	10	14	43
6						

3.

÷	20	4	28	12	36	44
4						

4. Write forty-nine thousand and sixteen as a numeral.

5. Complete this pattern:

5, 7, 8, 10, ☐ , ☐ , ☐

6. What comes next?

$\frac{78}{100}$ $\frac{79}{100}$ ☐

7. Fries are 90 cents, burgers $2.65. For $10 can I buy 3 burgers and 4 fries?

8. 0.05 as a percentage is:

9. Approximately what change should I get from $20 after spending $6.95 and $7.30?

10. Mum bought 4 m of fabric at $4.95 a metre. What change will she receive from a $50 note?

Measurement and Geometry

11. Is 2200 hours 2 am / 2 pm / 10 pm?

12. Gina filled a balloon with 560 mL of water. The balloon and water have a mass of:
(a) a little more than 560 g
(b) less than 560 g
(c) well over 600 g

13. 2 metres 45 cm can be written as ☐ m or ☐ cm.

14. 4 m
8 m²

This rectangle is 4 m long and has an area of 8 m². How wide is the rectangle?
1 m / 2m / 4m

15. I constructed an irregular solid using 27 centicubes, then put this shape into a jug holding 100 mL of water. The water level should now read:

16. Inside refrigerator is 3 °C. Outside refrigerator is 21 °C. What is the difference?

17. Which way—(horizontal / vertical / sloping)— would the cross-section of this solid have to be taken to form a circle?

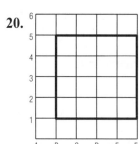

18. An angle of 137° is (acute / obtuse / reflex).

19. Name the most symmetrical 2D shape.

20.

Name the coordinates of the intersection of the diagonals of this square.

Statistics and Probability

21. This graph shows people's height compared to their age. Mary is short for her age. True or false?

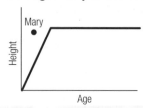

22. 10 red and some green counters were placed into a bag. How many green were put in if I have a one in two chance of drawing a red?

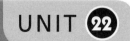

Cassan's lesson

Long ago there lived a beggar named Cassan. The only way he knew how to live was by begging for coins and food, or by stealing from those who had more than he. One day as he wandered through the market place he saw a traveller and his dog. Cassan knew the man was wealthy because of his fine clothes and the fat purse hanging from his belt. Cassan was very hungry. The purse looked even larger as he closed in on the stranger and reached out for it. He was about to grab the object of his desire when a strange voice said "Please do not steal my master's purse." The voice seemed to come from near his feet. Cassan looked down. It was the stranger's canine companion who was speaking. Despite being so startled Cassan blurted out, "I need money to buy food."

"My master provides me with food for the services I provide him," replied the dog. "Why do you not seek work and thus not steal?" Cassan replied that no one would give a beggar work. He could not believe it; here he was talking to a dog. "I too was once a beggar like you," the dog told Cassan, "but was turned into a dog for my evil deeds. Do not follow my path. Speak to my master and he will help you." Cassan nervously told the stranger what he had meant to do and how the dog had stopped him. The stranger replied, "You have done the right thing. Will you join me in my search for the wizard to turn my friend back into a human?" Cassan hesitated but he had no idea of the adventures that were yet to come.

Reading and Comprehension

1. What was the *object of his desire*? _____

2. In the story a word that also means 'dog' is used.
   This word is _____.

3. Why did the dog have the power of speech?
   (a) A wizard gave him the power.
   (b) He was a human once.
   (c) His master had taught him.
   (d) He was a very smart dog.

4. In your opinion this story is
   (a) the start of many adventures for Cassan.
   (b) how Cassan became a dog.
   (c) how Cassan saved the dog.
   (d) the only adventure Cassan had.

5. Which of these statements is not true?
   (a) Cassan hadn't eaten for days and was hungry.
   (b) The stranger's purse got bigger as Cassan approached.
   (c) The dog actually spoke to Cassan.
   (d) The dog believed that stealing was wrong.

Spelling and Vocabulary

Rewrite the misspelt words.

6. I have ninty cents to spend today. _____

7. Wich one do you want me to complete? _____

Circle the word that has the nearest meaning to the underlined word.

8. A solitary tree grew on the hill.
   (a) lone   (b) tall
   (c) shady   (d) stunted

9. Advertise your new play.
   (a) prepare   (b) practise
   (c) begin   (d) announce

Circle the correct word in brackets.

10. Glen gave out (one, won) last moan.

11. (Bares, Bears) hibernate during winter.

12. That's (right, wright).

Grammar and Punctuation

13. Add **phrases** to this sentence.

    The mouse _____ quickly
    scampered _____.

14. Punctuate and capitalise this sentence.

    when im in year eight ill be as big and strong as joshua hall

    _____

    _____

Mathematics

Number and Algebra

1.

+	7	4	1	5	0	26
6						

2.

−	15	11	17	9	13	74
8						

3.

×	2	6	0	4	8	12
2						

4. Write 94 049 in words.

5. Complete the pattern:

16, 21, 26, ⬚ , ⬚ , ⬚

6. Write the next fraction: $\frac{81}{100}$, $\frac{8}{10}$, ⬚

7. T-shirts are on special at $6.95. What notes will I need to buy 5 shirts?

8. Alana was offered 0.7 of a pizza or 75%. Which is the greater?

9. Round off 13 495 to the nearest thousand.

10. In a hall there are 800 seats arranged in 20 rows. How many seats are in each row?

Measurement and Geometry

11. Convert the analogue time to 24 hour digital.

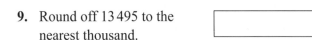

⬚ : ⬚

at night

12. Which unit (g / kg) has been left off each one?

(a)   (b)   (c)

13. 8 metres 9 cm in metres is written as: 8.9 m / 8.09 m / 8.90 m

14.  This square has an area of 4m². If I double the length of each side, I double the area.   True or false?

15. 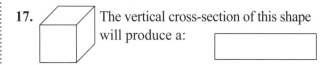 What is the volume of the stone?

16. If the temperature is 16 °C, it will have to rise ⬚ to reach 42 °C.

17. 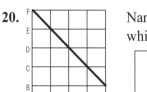 The vertical cross-section of this shape will produce a:

18. An angle greater than 180° but less than 360° is termed a ⬚ angle.

19. Which digits are symmetrical?

20. 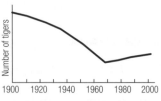 Name all of the points through which this line passes.

Statistics and Probability

21. This graph shows the population of tigers in India.

When do you think tigers became protected animals?

22. Some Year 5 children measured the length of their jumps: (a) 198 cm   (b) 185 cm
(c) 213 cm   (d) 174 cm   (e) 150 cm
Which jump is closest to the mean?

Lucky beans

In the city of Jerusalem during the Roman occupation of Israel in 36 BC lived a carpenter named Saul and his 16-year-old daughter Rebekkah. Saul was a compulsive gambler. He'd gamble away his money on any sort of contest. Sometimes he won, but usually he lost. Often he left Rebekkah with very little housekeeping money. This taught her to become efficient with the little she had. When Saul won, which was rare, he would buy Rebekkah gifts, for he was a loving father. Either way they had very little money.

One day at the local inn, he began to play against Marcellus, a wealthy Roman merchant. From that day on, Saul's luck deserted him. Eventually he lost everything: his furniture, his house and his tools of trade. He was destitute. Marcellus had met Rebekkah and was impressed by her. He thought she would make a good housekeeper. He pretended to pity Saul, and offered him a chance to win everything back. "Rebekkah's service for 5 years," he said, "against your losses."

So five years of Rebekkah's freedom depended on the throw of a die. Saul threw … and lost. That evening Rebekkah became Marcellus's bond servant. She accepted her misfortune quietly. She wiped away her tears and began work: she washed his clothes, cleaned his house and cooked his food. She also watched him gamble. He was as compulsive as her father. Yet he never lost an important bet! This puzzled Rebekkah. So she studied him carefully, his strengths and weaknesses, concluding that Marcellus was a cheat! He used loaded dice. Her father had been a fool to bet against him.

Reading and Comprehension

1. Why did Marcellus never lose an important bet?

   _____

2. Who was the more compulsive gambler:

   Saul or Marcellus? _____

3. Rebekkah was born in
   (a) 52 BC.   (b) 36 BC.
   (c) 20 BC.   (d) 16 BC.

4. Saul was a compulsive gambler. This means
   (a) he was a successful gambler.
   (b) he was a poor gambler.
   (c) he never won.
   (d) he could not control his gambling.

5. Number these sentences in order (1–4).
   (a) Eventually he lost everything.
   (b) Saul was a compulsive gambler.
   (c) Rebekkah became Marcellus's servant.
   (d) Sometimes he won but usually he lost.

Spelling and Vocabulary

Rewrite the misspelt words.

6. I'll try hard to rememember what you've said.

7. That will cost you a dolar and forty-five cents.

Circle the word that has the nearest meaning to the underlined word.

8. The keys were put in the custody of their owner.
   (a) care   (b) office   (c) safe   (d) pocket

9. That is the solution to the problem.
   (a) question   (b) answer   (c) idea   (d) start

Circle the correct word in brackets.

10. Don't (eat, ate) these berries.

11. One of the men (come, came) to meet us

12. "Welcome our (guest, guessed)," said mum.

Grammar and Punctuation

13. Change the underlined words into **pronouns**.

    Fred was sure that Fred had put Fred's skateboard away when Fred had come home.

    _____

    _____

14. Punctuate and capitalise this sentence.

    this said the hunter is the den of the lion

    _____

    _____

Mathematics

Number and Algebra

1. Start with the 6 in the centre of the spiral and continue clockwise to add 4 to each number till you reach the circle.

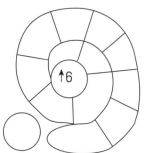

2. Start at 27 and subtract 3 from each number along the snake until you reach its head.

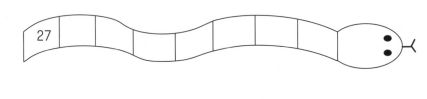

3. If $5 \times 8 = 40$ then $8 \times \boxed{} = 40$, $40 \div 8 = \boxed{}$, $40 \div 5 = \boxed{}$, $\frac{1}{8}$ of $40 = \boxed{}$, and $\frac{1}{5}$ of $\boxed{} = 8$.

4. Arrange these digits to form the greatest possible number: 4 , 7 , 8 , 3 , 0 $\boxed{}$

5. Complete this pattern: 16, 20, 25, 31, $\boxed{}$, $\boxed{}$, $\boxed{}$

6. Write these fractions on the cards from left to right in ascending order: 4 tenths , 44 hundredths, $4\frac{0}{10}$

7. Use your calculator to work out the missing amount on this petrol bowser.
Round your answer.

8. Here is a 20 litre drum of oil. 60% has been used. How much remains? (12 litres / 60% / 40 hundredths)

9. There are 157 apples in a basket. If they are packed in bags of 8, then I can pack approximately $\boxed{}$ bags.

10. Lucius is a student in an old Roman school. Help him do this sum in Roman numerals:

CCXXIX
+ CXXXVI
$\boxed{}$

Measurement and Geometry

11. It's half past seven at night or $\boxed{}$ (am/pm) or  or $\boxed{}$ (24 hour time).

12. An empty box has a mass of 110 g. If I pack six $\frac{1}{2}$ kg packets in the box, the box will have a total mass of $\boxed{}$ g.

13.  From this 4 metre roll of material I cut these pieces: 1.25 m, 80 cm, $\frac{1}{2}$ metre and 75 cm. How much is left of the roll?

14. Which of these processes would give me the area of a rectangle?
(a) Add up all of the sides.   (b) Add the length and the breadth and then double your answer.
(c) Multiply the perimeter by the length.   (d) Find the product of the length and breadth.

15. The measuring cylinder showed a volume of 105 mL. I added some centicubes. The reading became 127 mL. How many cubes did I add?

16. Cadia is sick in bed with a temperature of 3.7 degrees above normal (37 °C). What temperature is shown on the thermometer?
(a) 3.7 °C   (b) 40.7 °C (c) 103.7 °C

17. Here is a 3D drawing of a cone. Cross out the incorrect elevation.
   (a)   (b)   (c)

18. Use your protractor to measure the size of this angle.

19. Name the plane shape that has an infinite number of lines of symmetry.

20. 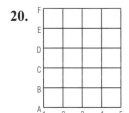 Plot the points (1, B) and (5, F). Join the points. Name the other points through which this line passes.

Statistics and Probability

21.  This graph shows us travelling one day. Circle the part of the graph that shows where you think we stopped for lunch.

22. These 3 coins were tossed. This is the result. What other results are possible?

History of the game

Hockey, claimed to be one of the first sports ever played, has two different forms—field hockey and ice hockey. The game is very closely associated with the Scottish game of shinty, the English bandy and the Irish hurling. All these games involve the use of a curved stick to hit a ball. The name hockey seems to have come from the French *hoquet*. This word means 'shepherd's crook', and the hockey stick is shaped very much like it.

The game of hockey goes back to the early days in a country called Persia (now known as Iran). It was also played by the ancient Greeks. We know this because archaeologists working on old walls in Greece found pictures of people playing hockey. The Romans learned it from the Greeks, then introduced it to countries they colonised.

Hockey was a favourite game of the American Indians. However, their game was quite rough and often turned into a riot. They did not wear any protective gear. Sticks were used to move other players out of the way of the ball. By the end of the game there were many injuries. The players, however, were quite content to forget the bruises and celebrate with a party. This was the tradition of the American Indians.

For a long time hockey was played without any definite rules. Any number of people could join in and there were no set positions like winger or centre-forward. Players would do anything to snatch the ball from each other, and games often ended up in wild brawls.

Gradually rules were introduced to eliminate the dangers. Players were not allowed to raise the head of their stick above their shoulders. This was one of the earliest rules. They were suspended from play if they hit an opponent with their stick or hand. Protective clothing was introduced to avoid injuries. Most players today wear mouthguards and shin-pads to lessen the risk of injury.

The Irish introduced the fearsome game of hurling to Australia during the goldmining era of the mid-1800s. This was eventually replaced with a game more like hockey. Ships from the Royal Navy used to visit Australia with hockey teams aboard. They were the first to play the game as an organised sport in Australia.

How to play hockey

The modern game of hockey is a fast and exciting game for both players and spectators. Each player uses a stick that has a flat side. The ball may only be hit with the flat side of the stick. The head of the stick is made of wood.

Games are played for two periods, each one lasting thirty-five minutes. Hockey requires many skills. Players must learn to use their sticks so that they can run with the ball.

English

Reading and Comprehension

1. When was hurling introduced into Australia?

   _____

2. In which country was hockey first played?

   _____

3. The word *hockey* comes from
   (a) the Scottish game of shinty.
   (b) the English game of bandy.
   (c) the French word *hoquet*.
   (d) the Irish game of hurling.

4. How is it known that ancient Greeks played hockey?
   (a) from writings in old books
   (b) from pictures found on walls by archaeologists
   (c) from famous stories
   (d) from old rule books

5. Number these versions of hockey (1–4) in the correct order of time when they were played.
   (a) the form played originally in Persia
   (b) the version played by the American Indians
   (c) the version played by the ancient Greeks
   (d) the first form played here in Australia

Spelling and Vocabulary

Rewrite the misspelt words.

6. By the end of the game their were many injeries.

   _____

   _____

7. Most players today where mouthguards and shin-pads to lesen the risk of injury.

   _____

   _____

   _____

Circle the word that has the nearest meaning to the underlined word.

8. The Irish <u>introduced</u> the game of hurling into Australia.
   (a) met   (b) brought in
   (c) were good at   (d) shook hands

9. <u>Archaeologists</u> found pictures of people playing hockey.
   (a) scientists who study old civilisations
   (b) doctors who study old people
   (c) people who like sport
   (d) people who study how sports developed

Circle the correct word in brackets.

10. Players are not allowed to (rays, raise) the sticks above their shoulders.

11. Our women's team won a gold (meddle, medal) at the Seoul Olympics.

12. Shin-pads and mouthguards (lesson, lessen) the risk of injury.

Grammar and Punctuation

13. Rewrite this sentence twice so that the underlined phrase is in a **different position** in the sentence each time.

    There are eleven players <u>in a hockey team</u>.

    (a) _____

    _____

    (b) _____

    _____

14. Rewrite this sentence with correct punctuation and capitalisation.

    the word hockey appears to have come from the french word hoquet which means shepherds crook

    _____

    _____

    _____

Mathematics

Number and Algebra

1.

+	1	5	0	9	6	33
8						

2.

−	7	8	4	12	9	66
4						

3.

÷	56	35	49	28	42	77
7						

4. Expand 66 161.

5. Complete the pattern.

12, 24, 36, _____ , _____ , _____

6. Write in order from smallest to largest.

$\frac{4}{10}$, $\frac{60}{100}$, $\frac{66}{100}$,

7. Julie had $78.45 in her purse.
She spent $29.50.
What amount has she now?

8. 5.53 − 3.68 =

9. Round off 4865 to the
nearest ten thousand.

10. What will 9 tins of spaghetti
at $0.92 each cost?

Measurement and Geometry

11. Write 9:42 am in
24 hour time.

12. Write four hundred and four
kilograms in shortened form.

13. There are _____ metres in a
kilometre.

14. Write seven hectares in
shortened form.

15. A solid with a volume of 27 cm³ will displace
_____ mL of water.

16. What temperature
is shown on this
thermometer?

17. Comment on
this drawing.

18. Through how many right angles does the minute
hand of a clock
turn from midday to
12:45 pm on the same day?

19. Complete this shape
using the line of
symmetry given.

20. Mark the cardinal points
on this diagram.

Statistics and Probability

21.

The graph shows the
growth of a plant. When
did the plant stop growing
in height?

22. There are four girls, named Jill, Maree, Luan and
Karlee. What are the chances of picking a girl
from the group and giving
her the right name?

Now's the Time!

The time to start a regular exercise program is when you are young. It should become an everyday habit while you are still at school. It is wise to choose an activity that you enjoy, or a few new activities for variety. Choose from any of these aerobic activities: running, skipping, cycling, aerobics, surfing, skiing, swimming, dancing.

Team sports such as basketball, netball, football, volleyball and soccer are good fun. They also build up the cardiovascular system, especially if your team trains together as well as playing together. Different activities suit different people. Whatever activity you choose, as long as it is vigorous it will help to strengthen your heart and improve your circulation.

Exercise actually helps you feel more energetic and the more you do, the easier it becomes. As you start to get fit you feel good about yourself. You can even make new friends.

Exercise strengthens your muscles, joints and bones as well as your heart. Almost everything in your body works better with exercise.

Once you are fit you need to make sure you stay fit. To do this, you have to keep up an active lifestyle. Remember you cannot store fitness. But if you become an exercise fan, staying fit will not be difficult. Your exercise time will be something to look forward to!

Reading and Comprehension

1. Fitness can be stored up in your body.

   True or false?

2. At what age should you begin regular exercise?

   _____

3. Exercise should be done
   (a) regularly.
   (b) every day.
   (c) when you play sport.
   (d) when you need to get fit.

4. Which of these statements is not true?
   (a) Different activities suit different people.
   (b) Exercise makes you tired.
   (c) Exercise strengthens bones.
   (d) Exercise should be a daily habit.

5. Number these statements in order (1–4).
   (a) Start exercising when you are young.
   (b) Make exercise a habit.
   (c) Keep up an active lifestyle.
   (d) Play sport or do an aerobic activity.

Spelling and Vocabulary

Rewrite the misspelt words.

6. I look forward to our holydays in December.

   _____

7. Mike's birthday is in march. _____

Circle the word that has the nearest meaning to the underlined word.

8. There is a <u>universal</u> demand for more food.
   (a) strong   (b) widespread
   (c) loud   (d) unusual

9. I could not see for the <u>haze</u>.
   (a) rain   (b) clouds
   (c) darkness   (d) distortion

Circle the correct word in brackets.

10. My dog (berries, buries) bones in Mum's garden.

11. Perspiration oozed from every (pour, pore).

12. It collapsed from the (sheer, shear) weight on it.

Grammar and Punctuation

13. Use the word *paste* in a sentence so that it is

    a **verb**. _____

    _____

14. Punctate and capitalise this sentence.

    is this said the hunter the den of the lion

    _____

Mathematics

Number and Algebra

1.

+	7	4	9	5	6	53
7						

2.

−	9	2	10	6	5	100
1						

3.

×	2	7	3	9	5	10
9						

4. Write one numeral for
6 + 20 + 300 +
4000 + 90 000

5. Complete the pattern:

60, 56, 52, ⬚ , ⬚ , ⬚

6. What comes next? 0.78 , 0.79 , ⬚

7. Dad's bank balance was $1874.
After he banked $169 his
balance was:

8. 7.24 + 1.89 = ⬚

9. Will a $50 note be enough to
buy 2 articles A $18.75 and
B $36.50? Estimate only.   Yes or no?

10. There were 962 sheep.
189 were added to the flock.
The total is now:

Measurement and Geometry

11. Write 20:24 in am/pm time.

12. 7265 grams = ⬚ kg

13. 10.4 km = ⬚ m

14. Circle the areas you'd measure in hectares.
   (a) a suburban yard   (b) a farm
   (c) a golf course

15. Write thirty-nine cubic
centimetres in shortened form.

16. Show 28 °C on this thermometer.

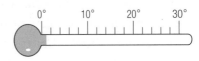

17. If a 1 m rule casts a 1 m shadow, how tall is the
tree?

1 m rule
1 m shadow
5 m shadow

18. Use your protractor to measure this angle.

19. Name the 2D shape that has uncountable lines of
symmetry.

20. Which direction is midway
between North and West?

Statistics and Probability

21.

Distance
Time

How many rest periods
did this driver take?

22. What are the possible outcomes when two discs
are drawn from a bag containing 10 red and
5 blue discs?

21 Alexis Drive
Farlington NSW 2174
24 April 2013

Dear Aunt Joan,

It has been some time since I have written to you because things haven't changed much. I'm in Year 5 this year. The work is harder but I am doing well. This year we have the chance to play interschool sport. I'm playing softball. Last match we played we had our first win against Avondale. We defeated them 8 to 6. I was named the best player for the match and got a certificate.

I'm really looking forward to next Wednesday— only three days to go—when I'll turn 10. I know I'll have to go to school but the excitement of opening my presents early is really growing. We are going to have a family dinner that night at Grandma's place. Mum said I could have some friends over for an afternoon tea and games—probably softball.

Mum and Dad said that next holidays we'll be going to Queensland. I really like surfing so the Gold Coast will be fantastic. Your town is on the way so I think we may drop in. Let us know if you'll be home in June or if you'll be on your trip to Canada. Write back after your trip and tell me what you saw. I wish I could go too. I look forward to your next letter and seeing you again.

Your nephew
Kristen

Reading and Comprehension

1. What is the date of Kristen's birthday?

   _____

2. Is Kristen male or female? _____

3. The 24th of April is a
   (a) Sunday.   (b) Monday.
   (c) Tuesday.   (d) Wednesday.

4. Why hasn't Kristen written to Aunt Joan recently?
   (a) There is no reason.
   (b) New things have happened.
   (c) New things haven't happened.
   (d) She's been too busy to write.

5. Number these events in order (1–4).
   (a) going to school
   (b) opening presents
   (c) sharing a meal with the family
   (d) sharing afternoon tea with friends

Spelling and Vocabulary

Rewrite the misspelt words.

6. My father was born in ninteen fifty-nine.

   _____

7. It's allready too late to go. _____

Circle the word that has the nearest meaning to the underlined word.

8. Those rocks are jagged.
   (a) black   (b) big   (c) dangerous   (d) sharp

9. The workers were united in their demands.
   (a) together   (b) arguing over
   (c) careless   (d) angry

Circle the correct word in brackets.

10. My (aunt, aren't) came to visit last week.

11. Dad puts too much (source, sauce) on his food.

12. What (weight, wait) of flour do you need?

Grammar and Punctuation

13. Insert the beginning words for these **phrases**.

    You will have to answer _____ your

    mother _____ your poor behaviour.

14. Punctuate this sentence in two diferent ways and capitalise it.

    bill said gino isnt living in henry street any more

    _____

    _____

    _____

    _____

Number and Algebra

1.

+	4	7	9	6	5	38
9						

2.

−	11	8	10	7	9	22
3						

3.

÷	24	36	54	12	6	48
6						

4. What is the value of the 8 in 20 897?

5. Complete the pattern:

3, 6, 10, ____, ____, ____

6. Change this fraction to a decimal.

$\frac{7}{10}$

7. What change will I get from $20 after spending $3.75 and $5.95?

8. $0.25 =$ ____ %

9. Round off 2.6 m to the nearest metre.

10. Share 364 lollies equally among 3 boys and a girl.

Measurement and Geometry

11. What is one hour after 11:15 am in 24 hour time?

12. 3.56 kg = ____ g

13. The scale on a map is 1 cm = 1 km. If A and B are 3 cm apart on the map, then in real life they are ____ apart.

14. Correct this statement if necessary. The paddock has an area of 5 ha^2.

15. A prism 3 cm × 5 cm × 2 cm has a capacity of:

16. Which object is the hottest?

28 °C   3 °C   54 °C

17. As you look down a road, the road appears to:
(a) widen   (b) get narrower
(c) stay the same width

18. Use your protractor to measure this angle.

19. Which quadrilateral has 4 lines of symmetry?

20. South-east is directly opposite to:

Statistics and Probability

21. At the end of the year, how much money will each child have received?

(a) ____
(b) ____
(c) ____
(d) ____
(e) ____

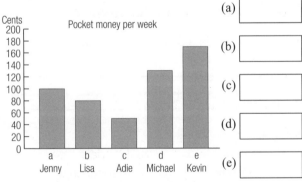

22. I have a ten times better chance of drawing a red marble than a white one. If there are 5 white marbles in the bag, then there must be ____ red ones.

Robert Louis Stevenson

In Edinburgh, Scotland, a boy was born on 13 November 1850. His parents called him Robert Lewis Balfour Stevenson. (When he was older he preferred to spell his name Louis.) He wasn't a strong child and was looked after by his nanny Alison Cunningham—Cummie as he called her. He loved stories and by the age of six had made up his mind to be a writer himself.

He loved make-believe. When he played with his toys he could almost persuade himself they were alive.

His parents wanted him to become an engineer like his father and his father before him. Robert studied law but never practised it. Instead he became a writer.

His health was never strong. He travelled and wrote widely until finally he settled in California where he become seriously ill and was nursed back to health by a woman who became his wife. On his recovery they purchased a sailing boat—sailing away, washing over the South Pacific Ocean for three years. He decided to make his home in Samoa. There he purchased land and lived three happy years.

When he died the whole island was plunged into grief. He was buried on the top of the hill near his home. In some ways Robert Louis Stevenson was indeed much like one of the characters in his famous book *Treasure Island*.

Reading and Comprehension

1. What was his nanny's nickname? _____

2. What does *washing over the South Pacific* mean to you?

   _____

3. Which of these statements about his childhood is false?
   (a) He had a great imagination.
   (b) He liked toys.
   (c) He visited distant lands.
   (d) His nanny helped him to get strong.

4. The people of Samoa were plunged into grief when he died. The Samoans were
   (a) unhappy.
   (b) sad.
   (c) very sad.
   (d) extremely saddened by his death.

5. Number these events in RL Stevenson's life (1–4).
   (a) graduated as a lawyer
   (b) became a writer
   (c) settled in California
   (d) decided to become a writer

Spelling and Vocabulary

Rewrite the misspelt words.

6. I carn't understand a word you say. _____

7. I cort a cold. _____

Circle the word that has the nearest meaning to the underlined word.

8. I listened to his explanation.
   (a) question   (b) problem   (c) reason   (d) story

9. The diagram was on the board.
   (a) lesson   (b) drawing   (c) story   (d) test

Circle the correct word in brackets.

10. That book is (new, knew).

11. The sky was dark (blew, blue).

12. It is not (right, write) to say that about your friend.

Grammar and Punctuation

13. Rewrite this sentence so that it happened **yesterday**.

    The bird lands on a branch, sings cheerfully and flies off again.

    _____

    _____

14. Punctuate and capitalise this sentence so that different speakers are used.

    the visitor said the gardener is in the hall

    _____

    _____

Number and Algebra

1.

+	7	4	9	8	1	64
1						

2.

−	11	7	4	2	6	61
2						

3.

×	5	3	7	4	8	12
5						

4. Which 6, A or B, has the
greater value in 26 016?
        A   B

5. Complete the pattern:

12, 10, 13,11, [   ] , [   ] , [   ]

6. Circle the fraction of greater value.

$\frac{6}{10}$ $\frac{6}{100}$

7. Two articles are $14.65 and $6.35.
How much more than $20
do I need to buy them?

8. 7% + 0.07 = [   ]

9. 7.05 L to the nearest litre is:

10. Half a drum contains 14.7 L.
When full it holds:

Measurement and Geometry

11. What is one hour before
13:05 in am/pm form?

12. If 1 kg of water has a volume
of 1 L, then 6.5 L of water
has a mass of:

13. 5647 m = [   ] km

14. Convert 50 000 square
metres to hectares.

15. A hollow prism 4 cm × 2 cm × 3 cm, if filled
with water, will hold [   ] mL.

16. Normal body temperature for
humans is (0 °C / 37 °C / 100 °C)?

17. These two trees look to be the same size,
but which is taller?

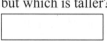

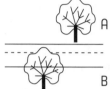

18. Use a protractor to
draw an angle of 40°.

19. This triangle has 3 equal sides.
Draw in the lines of symmetry.

20. If I turn 45° clockwise
from North, I'm facing:

Statistics and Probability

21.

(a) What is the average
    height of the children?
(b) How many children are
    above the average?

22. I was told that there were 60 blue and 2 green
counters in a box. Sixty times I drew out a
counter and put it back. Sixty times I drew a blue
one. My next draw will be a green one. Is this
guaranteed / possible / likely / impossible?

Homework

There are two schools of thought on homework. One says that homework is of great value because it provides revision of what has been done in class that day. It also provides the discipline of doing work unsupervised outside the school room. Parents, too, are given an idea of what is going on in the classroom and the standard their children are attaining. Some parents enjoy the opportunity to sit down with their children while they do homework and regard this as a valuable period when they can get a better idea of what is going on at school.

The other group states that homework is of little value and cites the following reasons to have homework abolished. Children work hard all day in class, so why do they need to work at home? Parents are busy people and have no time to supervise children doing homework. Children need time to relax, play and enjoy their childhood, and homework takes up this valuable time. Some teachers support this by saying homework must be corrected and this wastes teaching time. Children with learning difficulties have problems, so all homework does is reinforce the failures those children already experience every day.

Whether homework should be set or not is still a matter of debate. What's your position on this matter?

Reading and Comprehension

1. The statement ... *to have homework abolished* means _____.

2. Name one reason why homework is considered valuable. _____

3. Why do some parents like homework?
    (a) It keeps children busy.   (b) It's good for them.
    (c) It's a time when parents communicate with their children.   (d) Children need homework.

4. Correcting homework is considered a waste of time by
    (a) teachers.   (b) all teachers.
    (c) parents.   (d) some teachers.

5. Number these points supporting homework in the order presented (1–4).
    (a) Homework is a good communication time for parents and children.
    (b) Homework is a routine or discipline.
    (c) Homework revises school work.
    (d) Parents get to know their child's ability/standard.

Spelling and Vocabulary

Rewrite the misspelt words.

6. Mary dose much more to help than Jim.
7. Docter Ryan operates on cancer patients.

Circle the word that has the nearest meaning to the underlined word.

8. Please contribute to our fund.
    (a) help   (b) provide
    (c) control   (d) use

9. It was a vivid picture.
    (a) clear   (b) violent
    (c) pretty   (d) unusual

Circle the correct word in brackets.

10. (Some, Sum) sums are easier than others.

11. (Where, Wear) is your hat?

12. Tessa (nose, knows) what she is talking about.

Grammar and Punctuation

13. Rewrite this sentence so that it will happen **tomorrow**.

    At night I climbed into bed, closed my eyes and soon went off to sleep.

    _____

    _____

14. Punctuate and capitalise this sentence.

    from coopers creek burke wills king and gray set off for the gulf of carpentaria

    _____

    _____

    _____

Mathematics

Number and Algebra

1.

+	1	7	3	9	5	14
3						

2.

−	13	17	11	15	18	46
9						

3.

÷	15	35	25	45	5	55
5						

4. If I move a digit from one column to the column next to it on the left, I increase its value

   by [   ] times.

5. Count on in this series:

   492, 494, 496, [   ] , [   ] , [   ]

6. Which has the greater value:

   $\frac{4}{10}$ or 47 hundredths?

7. Lamb chops are \$2.99 a kg. What will 3 kg cost me?

8. $0.56 + 0.02 =$ [   ] %

9. 985×17 is roughly

10. 75% of my money is \$12. How much have I?

Measurement and Geometry

11.  Convert this time at night to 24 hour time.

12. Rewrite 7400 g in kg.

13. Cross out the ones I would **not measure** in kilometres.
    (a) thickness of a wall
    (b) distance from Sydney to Canberra
    (c) my own height

14. 3.6 ha = [   ] m²

15. A container holds 135 mL of dry sand. What is the cubic volume of this container?

16. 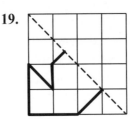 What is the difference between the temperature inside and outside the house?

17. If I put my hand between a light source and the wall (close to the light) the shadow of my hand is:
    (a) the same size as my hand
    (b) larger than my hand
    (c) smaller than my hand

18. Use a protractor to draw an angle of 140°.

19. 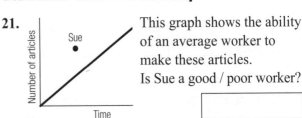 Complete the shape, given the line of symmetry.

20. 90° anti-clockwise from South-east is:

Statistics and Probability

21. This graph shows the ability of an average worker to make these articles. Is Sue a good / poor worker?

22. Gamer tossed a 20 cent coin 20 times and reported that it came down heads 20 times. Is this result unlikely / impossible / certain / likely?

English

Early days in Norfolk Island

Captain Arthur Phillip ordered the marines and convicts to disembark from the First Fleet on 26 January 1788 at Port Jackson. In early February Arthur Phillip ordered Philip King and 22 other persons (7 free men, 9 male convicts and 6 female convicts) to sail from Port Jackson in HMS *Supply* to establish a settlement on Norfolk Island. Philip King was well regarded, keen and considered the best person for the job.

With high hopes and some fear of the unknown, the party set off on 15 February, down the harbour and out into the Pacific Ocean. At 11 am on 29 February, Norfolk Island was sighted.

For five days they sailed around the island, exploring, looking for a safe place to land goods, livestock and passengers.

The landing was made and people set to work clearing ground to erect tents while the colours were hoisted. Soon, enough land had been cleared to plant seeds King had brought—cotton, wheat, corn, rice, vegetables, sugar cane and fruit trees. Planting was completed by 8 March. By 14 March shoots were well up. Then disaster—a strong south-west wind blew and every shoot was burnt by salt spray. A new area was cleared and replanted—these grew. Bananas were planted and flourished, but the island was not paradise.

Reading and Comprehension

1. *... the colours were hoisted*. What are *the colours*? _____

2. Why did they sail for five days around the island? _____

3. The first settlers on Norfolk Island were
   (a) convicts.
   (b) free men only.
   (c) the First Fleet.
   (d) 23 people, both convicts and free.

4. Which of these characteristics did Philip King display so as to be chosen to lead the settlement?
   (a) He was highly thought of.
   (b) He had the ability to do the job.
   (c) He was eager and keen to do the job.
   (d) He was afraid of the unknown.

5. Match these dates with the correct event.
   (a) 26 January (1) departure of HMS *Supply*
   (b) 15 February (2) completion of first plantings
   (c) 29 February (3) sighting of Norfolk Island
   (d) 8 March (4) landing of First Fleet at Port Jackson

Spelling and Vocabulary

Rewrite the misspelt words.

6. Everythink I do you say is wrong. _____

7. Your happyness is the most important thing. _____

Circle the word that has the nearest meaning to the underlined word.

8. He has a hearty laugh.
   (a) loud
   (b) unusual
   (c) foolish
   (d) vigorous

9. Mum will consider my question.
   (a) think about
   (b) answer
   (c) refuse
   (d) listen to

Circle the correct word in brackets.

10. Many (tales, tails) have been told about wild animals.

11. Give me (advise, advice) as to what to do.

12. The (souls, soles) of his shoes were worn through.

Grammar and Punctuation

13. Write the **plural** forms of these words.
    brother-in-law _____
    stepsister _____
    spoonful _____
    man-of-war _____

14. Punctuate and capitalise this sentence.
    what will i do inquired tasha when the jug is nearly full

Number and Algebra

1.

+	3	5	7	6	8	29
4						

2.

−	9	16	7	12	14	35
7						

3.

×	0	4	5	7	6	12
8						

4. What's the difference in value between the 4s in 40 492?

5. Count backwards in hundreds from 4362.

⬚ , ⬚ , ⬚ , ⬚

6. One hundred hundredths has a value of:

7. What actual change (notes and coins) will I get from $10 after I spend $1.98?

8. 3.25 kg − 1.87 kg =

9. If I divide 5879 by 6, my approximate answer is:

10. From a 25 kg bag of potatoes Mum used 6000 g. What weight of potatoes remains?

Measurement and Geometry

11. 25 to nine at night in 24 hour time is:

12. An empty bucket weighs 389 g. When full of water it weighs 7.389 kg. What is the mass of water in the bucket?

13. 1564 m + 2436 m = ⬚ km.

14. One ten thousandth of a hectare is:

15. To have the capacity of 1 L, the container must have a volume of:
10 cm³ / 100 cm³ / 1000 cm³

16. Before the rain it was 28 °C. After the rain the temperature dropped 9° to:

17. Draw the top view of a cricket stump.

18. Write the type of angle if its size is 132°.

19. Look at a human face. Is it truly symmetrical? Yes or no?

20. If ⟶ is North,
then | means:
↓

Statistics and Probability

21.
Which car covered the distance at the greater speed?

22. When a die is rolled, each number has a one in six chance of turning up. This means that I'll roll a six every six rolls. True or false?

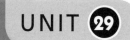
Hidden messages

When, on advertisements, we see nurses and teachers and they are all portrayed by women, the message we are being given is that these are women's jobs and that men do not do this sort of work. And when we see men being pilots, carpenters, business managers or doctors, we are being told that these are men's jobs; they are not for women.

It is the same with jobs around the house. Advertisements usually show Mum in the kitchen or the laundry talking about how good a soap powder or a dishwasher is. The hidden message is that housework is a woman's job, not a man's. Sometimes we will see a man doing housework, but he is usually shown to be helpless and not able to do it properly. This supports the view that it is women's work. The message is that Dad cannot do it properly because he is a male and housework is not a male job. These messages are known as stereotyping.

There would be nothing wrong with these hidden messages if it was true that some sorts of jobs are for women and other sorts of jobs for men. But it is not true. Women can work in tough jobs and gentle jobs—they can be pilots, dentists, truck drivers and mechanics as well as nurses and telephonists. And so can men. In fact most people can do any kind of work they set their minds to and it does not matter if they are male or female.

Reading and Comprehension

1. What is stereotyping? _____

_____

2. People can do any type of job provided they put

their _____ to it.

3. Housework is a woman's job. This is
   (a) true because women do it well.
   (b) because men are helpless.
   (c) stereotyping.
   (d) because only mums do it.

4. Which of these statements is true?
   (a) Men can't do housework.
   (b) Women can do tough jobs and so can men.
   (c) There are no women pilots.
   (d) Companies only employ female secretaries.

5. Which of these statements about advertising is true?
   (a) There's nothing wrong with hidden messages.
   (b) Women's minds are better than men's minds.
   (c) Stereotyping is common in advertisements.
   (d) There's nothing wrong with stereotyping.

Spelling and Vocabulary

Rewrite the misspelt words.

6. A lasar light was used to remove the tattoo.

_____

7. It's nearly three oclock. _____

Circle the word that has the nearest meaning to the underlined word.

8. We must alter our plans.
   (a) explain   (b) change
   (c) decide on   (d) think over

9. Puppies can be really annoying.
   (a) a loss   (b) a threat
   (c) a nuisance   (d) a joy

Circle the correct word in brackets.

10. Your (hair, hare) is quite long.

11. I like (fair, fare) hair more than dark hair.

12. He has (drank, drunk) too much wine.

Grammar and Punctuation

13. Write a sentence in which *flour* is used as a **verb**.

_____

14. Punctuate and capitalise this sentence.

my older brother alfred works as a salesperson for david jones

_____

_____

Number and Algebra

1.
+	6	2	0	8	4	19
2						

2.
−	7	6	9	5	8	54
5						

3.
÷	16	32	8	64	0	96
8						

4. Which digit in 16 589 has the least value?

5. Complete the pattern:

720, 820, 920, ☐ , ☐ , ☐

6. Take one hundredth from 0.7.

7. (a) 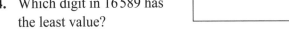 (b) Which is the cheaper per kg?

20 kg $5.20   3 kg $0.80

8. 2.24 m + 4.59 m =

9. Round off 7.56 to the nearest whole number.

10. Share out $21 so that Paul gets $1 more than Pedro and Lu receives $2 more than Pedro.

Measurement and Geometry

11. Convert 14:40 to written analogue form.

12. 3 kg 140 g= ☐ g = ☐ kg

13. 5 km − 500 m = ☐ km

14. This irregular block of land contains 10 000 m² or ☐

15. 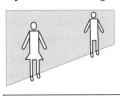 Volume = ☐
4 cm 5 cm 3 cm
Capacity = ☐

16. Match these:

(a) Water boils   (1) 37 °C

(b) Normal human body temperature   (2) 0 °C

(c) Water freezes   (3) 100 °C

17. Jim and Jane are the same height. What can you say about the height of the wall?

18. Draw a reflex angle of 210°.

19. Many objects made by people are symmetrical but few natural objects are truly symmetrical. True or false?

20. ↓ refers to the West,

therefore → means:

Statistics and Probability

21.  On which day was the highest temperature recorded?

Degrees
M T W T F

22. Explain why, when 2 dice are rolled, it is easier to score 7 than 12.

Holden car

The Holden was the first fully Australian car. Its story began in 1854 when James Alexander Holden arrived in Adelaide. In two years he had opened his own leather business. By the end of the 1870s he and his son were making upholstery (seat covering and padding) for horse-drawn carriages as well as hardware and other things. After the First World War they began building car bodies (but not engines), and in 1923 they agreed to make car bodies for General Motors, a very large American car company that was operating in Australia.

However, 1930 was a bad year for Western businesses. Many companies lost a lot of money and had to close. The Holden company was only saved because it joined together with General Motors. This gave it more money but the Holden family no longer completely owned it. After the Second World War, General Motors-Holden, launched the first all-Australian car known as the 48/125. It was a huge success, and immediately became Australia's top selling car. The engine was smooth and quiet. It did not use up petrol as quickly as other cars did. The acceleration was excellent, and it also drove well over rough roads.

Since 1948, many different Holden models have been manufactured. The most successful model in recent years has been the VN Commodore. In 1988 this car won Australia's three major Car of the Year Awards. It looks certain that the famous Holden name will live on for many years to come.

Reading and Comprehension

1. In which year did the VN Commodore win three awards? _____

2. The company General Motors is based in which country? _____

3. In which year did James Alexander Holden begin business in Australia?
   (a) 1854   (b) 1856   (c) 1970   (d) 1923

4. In 1930 the Holden company was saved because
   (a) General Motors gave Holden money.
   (b) many companies closed.
   (c) the Holden company was sold.
   (d) many other companies lost money.

5. Number these statements in order (1–4).
   (a) Holden made car bodies for General Motors.
   (b) Holden sold the first Australian-made car.
   (c) The Holden family made upholstery.
   (d) The Holden name will live on in Australia.

Spelling and Vocabulary

Rewrite the misspelt words.

6. This is a quite place in which to rest. _____

7. I'm tried and I'm going to bed. _____

Circle the word that has the nearest meaning to the underlined word.

8. The dog emerged from the room.
   (a) appeared   (b) ran   (c) sprang   (d) swam

9. I don't like being jostled in a crowd.
   (a) pushed   (b) spoken to
   (c) helped   (d) punched

Circle the correct word in brackets.

10. When the (tied, tide) went out the boat was stranded.

11. (Hear's, Here's) hoping you are well soon.

12. I like the smell of your new (sent, scent).

Grammar and Punctuation

13. Add the **phrases** *with a video camera* and *across the creek* to this sentence.

    The elderly gentleman approached the narrow bridge.

    _____

    _____

14. Punctuate this address correctly.

    mrs cl fellows coomoomie ms 48 glen innes 2568

    _____

    _____

    _____

Mathematics

Number and Algebra

1. 7 plus 3 = [   ] , add 4 = [   ] with 5 more = [   ] and 9 give a total of [   ] .

2. Find the answer when 8, 6, 4, 2, 3, and then 5 are taken from 42.   [   ]

3. If I add 7 six times I will have a total of   [   ]

4. A one placed in the hundreds column has (more / less) value than a nine in the tens column.   [   ]

5. Continue the pattern: 5 , 10 , 20 , 35, [   ] , [   ] , [   ]

6. One tenth take away one hundredth leaves [   ] .

7.

toy car	doll	cricket bat	ball
$18.95	$25.50	$17.20	$8.75

If I buy one of each, how much change will I get from $100?

[   ]

8. If
$$\begin{array}{r} 3.43 \\ + 5.68 \\ \hline 9.11 \end{array}$$
then
$$\begin{array}{r} 34.3 \\ + 56.8 \\ \hline \end{array}$$
[   ]

Explain how you can do this without recalculating.

[   ]

9. Mani looked at the change in his pocket. He stared at the coins and said, "I had a $20 note and no coins. I bought a book for about $9.95 and a present for $6.20. I have about [   ] left."

10.

Only 10% of the coffee remains in the tin. What is this remaining amount in grams?   [   ]

Measurement and Geometry

11. [**20:40**] is the same as [**   :   **] (am/pm) and

12.

1 kg

4 × 200 g masses

From these two weightings, what can we say about the mass of the pineapple?

[   ]

13.  1 Million Millimetre Race

Give this distance in:
(a) metres

(b) kilometres

14. Uncle Bob's farm has an area of 7 and a half hectares.
That is 7500 square metres / 75 000 square metres / 70 000.5 m².

15. I have two blocks of metal. If I put each into similar measuring jugs containing the same amount of water, which one will raise the water level the most?

16. What is the temperature shown on this thermometer?

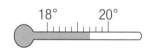

17. By looking, not measuring, which is the longer line?

18. Honeycomb from bees is made up from tessellated 3D shapes. Which of these shapes do they use?

19. Gum trees are seldom symmetrical but Christmas trees (pine trees) are. Comment on this statement.

20. If  represents North, show:

East	West	South

Statistics and Probability

21.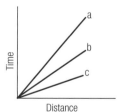

This graph shows the time it took to cover the same distance.
Match the lines with these: Horse, Triathlete and 4WD.

22. When two dice are rolled, there is a better chance of getting an even number than an odd number. Prove / disprove this statement.

Australia

Australia is the world's largest island, the fifth largest nation in the world and, after Antarctica, it is the driest. Australia is a land of climatic extremes where temperatures can be both very low and very high in different places at the same time of year. It has been inhabited by Aboriginal people for over 40 000 years. The arrival of Europeans just over 200 years ago had a dramatic effect on the hunting and gathering society of Aboriginal people.

Aboriginal people survived successfully on the foods of the bush; collecting berries, hunting birds and other animals, and fishing in the rivers and sea. About one or two hours each day were spent gathering enough food for the day.

Aboriginal people were like 'bush detectives' when searching for food. The sight of mosquitoes hovering over the hollow of a tree generally led them to a possum. Honey was located by gluing a small feather to a native bee, which would be followed back to its hive and its hoard of honey. Small birds were caught by smearing perches with a sticky fig sap.

European people arrived from England and tried to establish a lifestyle similar to the life back home. They planted English crops and introduced hoofed animals such as cattle and sheep. Not being prepared for the hot Australian climate and poor soils, they soon experienced food shortages. The severe food shortages could have been avoided if the early settlers had taken greater notice of the way Aboriginal people collected their food.

Bush foods were occasionally used by the early settlers, convicts and explorers to supplement their diets. The desert survival of Ludwig Leichhardt, an early Australian explorer, can be attributed to bush foods. Leichhardt ran out of sugar, tea and flour long before he reached his destination while exploring northern Australia. He readily experimented with bush foods and made meals of crows, dingoes, pigeon feet, native fruits, tubers, gums, emu gizzards and lizards.

The early settlers used bush foods to make jams and preserves. The English always enjoyed a cup of tea, but did not bring enough with them to Australia. The early settlers, in a desperate bid to make a cup of tea, used a native plant called Leptospermum to make tea. This plant is commonly called tea-tree.

Over time, the early settlers improved farming methods and planted crops more suited to Australian conditions. These included wheat, and fruits and vegetables such as apricots, cherries, peaches, citrus, pumpkins, potatoes, cabbages, beans and peas. The diet of the early settlers was dominated by beef and lamb. Damper, a bread substitute, was often eaten with these meat dishes. Meat dishes still dominate the Australian diet, although many people are now eating more vegetables than in the past.

Reading and Comprehension

1. The Australian bread substitute is called

   _____ .

2. How did Leichhardt survive in the desert?

   _____

3. The hunting and gathering of the Aboriginal people was most affected by
   (a) Australia being so dry.
   (b) the arrival of Europeans.
   (c) 40 000 years of food consumption.
   (d) changes in temperature.

4. Early European settlers could have avoided food shortages by
   (a) learning from the Aboriginal people.
   (b) bringing better seeds for their crops with them.
   (c) fertilising poor soils.
   (d) bringing more cattle and sheep.

5. Match these food sources with the way the Aboriginal people found them.

   (a) possums   (1) by smearing sap on branches
   (b) honey   (2) by looking for hovering mosquitoes
   (c) birds   (3) by gluing a feather on a bee

Spelling and Vocabulary

Rewrite the misspelt words.

6. About one or too hours a day where spent hunting and gathering food.

   _____

   _____

   _____

7. Many people are now eating moor vegtables than in the passed.

   _____

   _____

Circle the word that has the nearest meaning to the underlined word.

8. Aboriginal people survived successfully on the foods of the bush.
   (a) lived   (b) ate
   (c) gathered   (d) hunted

9. Severe food shortages could have been avoided by the early settlers.
   (a) greater
   (b) lessened
   (c) kept out of the way
   (d) much worse than expected

Circle the correct word in brackets.

10. The Australian climate was (to, too, two) hot.

11. The later settlers planted crops more (sooted suited) to the climate.

12. (Meet, Meat) dishes still dominate the Australian diet.

Grammar and Punctuation

13. Rewrite these sentences so that they will happen **tomorrow**.

   Aboriginal people survived on bush foods. They gathered berries, hunted animals and caught fish.

   _____

   _____

   _____

14. Rewrite this sentence with correct punctuation and capitalisation.

   ludwig leichhardt an australian explorer survived in the desert by eating native birds animals and fruit reported jane

   _____

   _____

   _____

© 1997 Harval Pty Ltd and Pascal Press
Reprinted 1998, 1999, 2000, 2001, 2002, 2003, 2005, 2006, 2007, 2008 (twice), 2009, 2010, 2011, 2012

Updated in 2013 for the Australian Curriculum

Reprinted 2014, 2015, 2016, 2018, 2019, 2020 (twice), 2021, 2022

ISBN 978 1 86441 276 5

Pascal Press
PO Box 250
Glebe NSW 2037
(02) 8585 4050
vvww.pascalpress.com.au

Publisher: Vivienne Joannou
Project editor: Mark Dixon
Australian Curriculum updates edited by Frances Wade and answers checked by Peter Little
Typeset by JMV Computer Services and Grizzly Graphics (Leanne Richters)
Cover by DiZign Pty Ltd
Printed by Vivar Printing/Green Giant Press

Acknowledgements
The following sources for material are kindly acknowledged:

Additional Fables by Mary Small

My Diary by Jenny Jarman-Walker

Strange Mysteries by Rachel Collinson

The Tooth Book by Viki Wright

Puppets by Carole Hooper

Tell Me How by Mike Callaghan et al

Antarctica by John Collerson

Radio Current Affairs by Elizabeth Halley

Earth First by Jenny Dibley and David Bowden

Hoosh! The Story of Camels in Australia by Keren Lavelle

Kites by Jenny Dibley and David Bowden

Technology for the Environment by Mike Callaghan and Peter Knapp

Spacescape by Karl Kruszelnicki

Saving Widlife by Edel Wignell

Sports in the Making by Shane Power

Hearty Facts by Shane Power

Not Another Ad! by John Fitzgerald

Made for Australia by Judith Kendra

What's Cooking? by Kerrie Bingle et al